Changing classroom cultures:
anti-racism, politics and schools

Changing classroom cultures:
anti-racism, politics and schools

Debbie Epstein

LEARNING
RESOURCES
CENTRE

Trentham Books

First published in 1993 by Trentham Books Limited

Trentham Books Limited
Westview House
734 London Road
Oakhill
Stoke-on-Trent
England ST4 5NP

British Library Cataloguing in Publication Data
A catalogue record for this book is available from the British Library

ISBN: 0 948080 65 5

Cover design by Judith Paton

Designed and typeset by Trentham Print Design Ltd, Chester
and printed in Great Britain by BPCC Wheatons Ltd, Exeter.

Contents

Acknowledgements

This book is based on the work I did for my doctoral thesis as the Department of Cultural Studies, Birmingham University. I would like to thank the following people for their support during my work for the thesis and when I was turning it into a book:

I could not have had a better teacher than my Ph.D. supervisor, John Gabriel, whose support was constant and who managed to challenge and question my work without ever making me feel inadequate.

Alison Sealey has been both a colleague and friend. Working with her has made me think and rethink. Her support — particularly at points when I had a crisis of confidence — has been invaluable.

David Ruddell was both a colleague and a friend. He supported and encouraged my work. His death in June 1990 represented a loss which I still feel.

The willingness of my colleagues in the multicultural support service and the many other teachers and children with whom I worked to co-operate with my research made it all possible. I have not been able to name them for reasons of confidentiality, but I owe them a huge debt of gratitude.

Many colleagues and friends have discussed with me the ideas in book and have read and commented upon various drafts of different chapters of both thesis and book, in particular: Stephen Ball, Diane Harris, Richard Johnson, Mary Kehily, Helen Kennedy, Paul Light, Beverley Naidoo, Thomas Ponniah, Iram Siraj-Blatchford, John Siraj-Blatchford, Deborah Steinberg. Also my students at Birmingham University and Birmingham Polytechnic, on whom I have tried the ideas in the book.

The women in my women's group — Kate Corr, Mary Kehily, Libby Kerr, Christine Lewis, Birgit Reinel and Deborah Steinberg — who have given me unstinting support and friendship and with whom I have discussed my knottiest problems.

Gillian Klein has been more than patient as editor. Her unfailing optimism and friendship have helped me finish the task.

There have been many other people who have helped me in a number of ways: in particular, Grahame Cooper helped me survive some painful times; Rona Epstein and Diana Paton willingly took on the tedious task of proof-reading my thesis.

Needless to say, none of these people is responsible for any of the faults which remain in the book — these are, I am afraid, all my own work!

CHAPTER ONE

INTRODUCTION

Changing Classroom Cultures is the result of my thinking and practice over a number of years during which I was head of an infant department in a large junior and infants school and, later, Teacher Adviser for Race Equality dealing with predominantly white primary schools in a large industrial city. During this period, I found it increasingly important to think about the complexities of racism, sexism and heterosexism[1] both in my classroom practice and in my analysis of strategies for change. Such complexities can be seen in any classroom, whether primary or secondary and regardless of the racial or class mix of children attending the school.

Consider the following hypothetical, but realistic scenarios, which could have taken place in virtually any of the schools I worked in as a teacher or Teacher Adviser.

1. The class is a well-organised and happy Year R class, where anti-sexist education has reached a high level of development. Some children are working with the teacher. Others are engaged in various activities including imaginative play, using construction toys, painting, doing puzzles and playing board games made by the teacher.

    As the children work and play, the teacher notices that one of the boys is regularly interfering with the activities of a little girl who is trying to build a machine out of meccano. Each time the girl reaches over to get a particular piece of meccano, the boy grabs it from her, saying, 'That's mine'. When the girl tries to get one of the pieces back, the boy says, in a gloating voice, 'I've got it'. The teacher goes over to the pair and is about to intervene, when the girl says, vehemently, 'Well, blackies can't play with this!'

2. In the playground of a middle school, two white girls in Year 7 shout at some boys 'F*** off, Pakis'. The teacher on playground duty overhears them and, horrified, is about to tell them off. Just before the teacher reaches the group, the boys turn on the girls, with the taunt 'Lezzies, lezzies!'

1

3. Two teachers are having a discussion in the staffroom which goes like this:

    A: I'm not happy about the fact that it's always the black boys who are chosen for the football team. It just feeds the stereotype of blacks being good at sport.

    B: Well, what're you saying ... shouldn't we choose them if they're the best players?

    A: No, it's not that, but why're they the best? That's what I want to know.

    B: Maybe it's chance, I dunno. But anyway, if we didn't choose the best players just because they're black, what would that be except discrimination, racial discrimination?

    A: Maybe, but why is it that most of our black kids don't seem to be doing particularly well at anything else?

4. In a staff meeting, teachers are discussing the possible effects of the implementation of the National Curriculum on their equal opportunities practices. One teacher expresses the opinion that there will no longer be time for attention to equality issues, and another disagrees, saying that equality should underpin everything they do. The head points out that the school's Governors will need to be convinced and that, in her view, the results in the Standard Assessment Tasks (SATS) are all-important because of the possible effects of results on school numbers.

These small, fictional incidents — which are, however, drawn from actual experiences — illustrate some of the complexities which face teachers trying to deal adequately with issues of inequality in their schools and classrooms. How can teachers decide, in situations where abuse and counter-abuse takes place, whether it is more urgent or important to deal with (in the examples given) racism, sexism or homophobia? Or should they try to deal with whichever forms of abuse appear simultaneously? In this book, I will be arguing that judgements about questions such as these need to be made with full knowledge of the particular situations and that there are no ready-made or easy answers. Although incidents such as the first two need to be dealt with immediately, it is not just in instant reactions to those incidents that successful approaches to developing anti-racist and anti-sexist education arise. Equally, in relation to the third vignette, of the discussion between two teachers, the answer that they should be dealing with the institutional racism in their school which has given rise to the situation described may be accurate but will not help them come to a conclusion over their immediate course of action. Neither are there any 'off the peg' answers to perceived problems in combining the demands of the National Curriculum and Assessment with those of education for equality. However both the curriculum (hidden and

2

overt) and the organisation of educational institutions are important part of developing education for equality. I will be returning to these matters in chapters 5 and 7.

Starting points

This book is about the search for some of the answers, or rather, for ways of approaching the questions raised by the anecdotes above. It starts from a political premise — that developing effective forms of anti-racist education (and of education for equality in general) and finding ways of empowering black people (and allowing them to empower themselves) are desirable. It is, therefore, not an intervention into debates about whether anti-racist education is necessary. My intention is, rather, to explore possible strategies for effective anti-racist education — particularly in predominantly white primary schools — and the macro- and micro-political factors influencing their development.

There has been a tendency in recent years to decry the role of theory in education. Courses of both initial teacher education and in-service education of teachers have been under pressure to adopt 'tips for teachers' approaches. It is, of course, a proper part of such courses, and of books like this one, to provide examples of classroom practice and to discuss practical problems and their solutions. However, all such practical examples and suggestions are, inevitably, based on some form of theory or way of making sense of the world and one's experience.

This theory may take the form of 'common-sense' or it may be made explicit. I would argue that 'common-sense' theorisations are dangerous for, in adopting them, we fail to think about what we are doing and why. Furthermore, if we do not develop explicit theories, then our ways of dealing with situations like those outlined above will always be purely reactive. It is possible to deal with complex events and situations adequately only if we have some kind of understanding of their complexity.

Therefore, although a large part of this book will consist of case studies of particular schools and teaching approaches, there will also be chapters which discuss the theoretical understandings which I have reached, through practice and reflection on practice and on which I tried to base my practice as teacher, Head of Infants and Teacher Adviser.

Theoretical frameworks and everyday life

As argued above, people understand their everyday experience through theoretical frameworks, which may or may not be consciously acknow-ledged. This has implications for forms of practice adopted. If, for example, teachers work on the assumption that children have an innate potentiality to develop in certain ways, which can be either nurtured or stunted (the common-sense assumption of many versions of 'child-centred' education — see also chapter 6), they will adopt a different set of teaching strategies than those teachers who assume that children are 'blank sheets' waiting to be written upon or 'empty vessels' waiting to be filled up (the common-sense assumption underlying many versions of formal pedagogy). Equally, if the underlying assumption about racism is that it is a result of ignorance, a different strategy for anti-racist education will be adopted than if it is conceived of as being something to do with institutional structures, or prejudice, or some combination of these. Consequently, I have tried to make explicit both my understandings of the ways in which racism works (in chapter 2) and my theoretical understandings of teaching and learning (in chapter 6).

People do not develop their theoretical perspectives as an intellectual exercise which is unrelated to their everyday experience. There is a dialectical relationship between theory and practice, in which each affects the other. As pointed out above, theory, even when unstated, will influence practice but, at the same time, the people's experiences (in this book, those of teachers and children in the classroom) will impact upon the explanations they give themselves for events. Since all experience (and therefore all thinking) takes place in specific contexts which have political, social, psychological and emotional dimensions, it is important to take these into account when trying to understand our everyday experience. This is not an easy undertaking, for it is not possible to stand outside our lives or the cultures which we inhabit. However it is possible to reflect on our positions and everyday experiences. It is, therefore, important to recognise clearly our positionality in relation to others, both generally and in particular contexts, and to ask questions about how this affects our views, explanations and practices.

Troyna and Hatcher (1992), in their useful discussion of 'flash points' for racist incidents in schools (pp. 39-47), suggest that there are eight levels of analysis necessary:

Structural: The differential relations of power and structurally induced conflict between groups perceived as racially different in society.

Political/ideological: Prevailing systems in play at the time of the incident. On the one hand, racism: justified in terms of the current *zeitgeist.* On the other, anti-racism: defended in terms of egalitarian ideals.

Cultural: The level of lived experience and common-sense understanding within the locality and community, especially as these are refracted through the family and its networks.

Institutional: The ideologies, procedural norms and practices which are promoted, sanctioned and diffused by the school.

Sub-cultural: The children's sub-cultural worlds.

4

Biographical: Those factors and characteristics which are specific to the individuals involved in the incident.

Contextual: The immediate history of a racist incident.

Interactional: The actual event/incident; what was done, what was said.

(p. 41)

I would suggest that it is not just for the understanding of racist incidents that we need to consider these different levels, but also for the analysis of social relations in general, of change and of the development of appropriate strategies to combat inequalities. In writing this book, I have therefore considered the macro-political context (chapters 3 and 4), the micro-politics of schools, and hence what Troyna and Hatcher have called 'cultural' and 'institutional' levels (in chapter 5) as well as the immediate classroom cultures and relationships, which include the sub-cultural, biographical, contextual and interactional levels (in chapter 7). It is important to note that, although these are, for convenience, largely separated in the discussion, they are not separate in our lived experience. They are intertwined and react with each other to produce particular situations.

Consequently, each individual situation in particular schools and classrooms is different. This does not, of course, mean that it is impossible to find ways of understanding them, but that any analysis must take place at the particular, micro-level as well as at the more general level. Every school and classroom is individual and unique, but there are also similarities between them and any strategy for change must take into account both the differences and the similarities. I would, therefore, hope that readers of this book will be actively engaged in considering the relationship of their own situations to those described here and will be able to draw out of the book some theoretical understandings of race and education and, as a result, some strategies for their own practice.

Teaching and research — teaching as research — research as teaching

Theory and practice

The field work for this book was carried out while I was head of an Infant Department in a large primary school and, subsequently, teacher adviser for race equality working in predominantly white schools in a large industrial city. The questions I was interested in arose directly from my needs as a teacher and a teacher adviser. In my work, I have drawn on theoretical understandings of child development and of a pedagogy which emphasises the social context of learning and seeks to democratise classroom practice through negotiation and collaborative work. It was in this area of research

5

that I found my role of teacher-as-researcher/researcher-as-teacher particularly valuable. I was already accustomed, as a practitioner, to taking account of research evidence in reflecting on my teaching. However, the further step of using practice as a way of reflecting on theoretical understandings was an important one. Others have written of the importance for teachers of developing theoretical understandings and being able to distance themselves from the immediate pressures of their day- to-day concerns in discussion of theoretical perspectives with colleagues (for example, Carrington and Short 1989, p. 154; Nixon 1985, p. 166). However, I would wish to add to this perspective the idea that reflection on practice is of as much benefit to the researcher wishing to develop and refine theory as it is to the teacher wishing to improve classroom practice.

The politically committed researcher

As stated above, the questions asked derived from my needs as a practitioner and activist. I believe that there are important consequences of a decision either to present research as divorced from politics (which remains conventional in social sciences) or to attempt to use research as a tool for political change (which is what I have done). It is not enough simply to condemn racism, or to do academic research relating to issues of race. Reflective intervention to combat it is also necessary. The questions asked by researchers and the discourses in which they engage are, inevitably, political. In any research project, the decision about which questions to ask is a political one, because it contains within it a judgement about the relative importance of different issues. During the course of research, the way the questions are answered is also political (see also Ben-Tovim et al 1986, chapter 1).

The political nature of such decisions is, perhaps, most obvious in the social sciences, but applies, too, to the so-called 'hard' sciences.[2] Stephen Jay Gould has shown the political nature of research in the biological sciences and statistics. In his book, *The mismeasure of man* (sic) (1981), Gould points out that:

> Science, since people must do it, is a socially embedded activity. ... Facts are not pure and unsullied bits of information; culture also influences what we see and how we see it. ...
>
> (pp. 21-22, Pelican edition)

Similarly, Rose et al (1984) argue that '... at any historical moment, what pass as acceptable scientific explanations have both social determinants and social functions.' (p. 33)

Within the social sciences, the political nature of research may be more or less obvious — and how obvious it is may change with time.[3] Bowlby (1951), for example, considered his research to be neutral and objective, and it was accepted as such, with important political results, by the scientific community and such influential bodies as the World Health Organisation. However, his views about 'maternal deprivation', which had clear implications for the possibility of gender equality, were later — under the impact of feminism — reassessed and found to be seriously flawed (see, for example, Clarke-Stewart 1988, Lloyd et al 1991). On the other hand, feminist research in the social sciences and much research in the area of race acknowledges clearly that such knowledge cannot be separated from politics.

The feminist philosopher of science, Sandra Harding (1991) is critical of versions of scientific and social scientific research 'requir[ing] the elimination of all social values and interests from the research process and the results of research' (p. 144). She points out that to discover that any form of human knowledge-seeking could 'defy historical 'gravity' and fly off the earth, escaping entirely their historical location' would be cause for considerable alarm amongst the scientific community, for 'it would appear to defy principles of 'material' causality upon which the possibility of scientific activity itself is based' (p. 145). She calls, instead, for research which, in acknowledging its political basis, examines the 'powerful background beliefs' that inevitably shape research in both natural and social sciences since they are constructed through and within particular cultures and historical locations.

This book is based on research for my doctoral thesis (Epstein 1991a). The project took the form of action research — that is, working collaboratively with teachers and children in schools to develop effective forms of anti-racist pedagogy and for school change. I recorded my findings on a day-to-day basis in records and evaluations of classroom work. I also kept a detailed research diary recording interactions in classrooms, staffrooms and meetings at work. Another research method was to use interviews with teachers (including heads and deputies). As my research proceeded, I also found it necessary to examine the wider political context and media representations of issues of race, racism and anti-racism for, to misquote Donne, 'no school is an island' and what happens in schools is inextricably linked with the wider context, with influences going both ways, from macro- to micro- and vice versa.

References for Chapter 1

1. 'Racism' is defined in chapter 2. I would define 'sexism' and 'heterosexism' as those processes and practices which disadvantage women and lesbians and gay men and which maintain the relative power of men and heterosexuals respectively.

2. AIDS activists, for example, have pointed out how political decisions about the classification of illness as being symptomatic of AIDS have been. The exclusion from the definition of AIDS of certain illnesses specific to women has obscured the fact that women become infected more easily than men through heterosexual penetrative intercourse — which has had serious implications for health promotion amongst women; diminished the amount of research done on AIDS-related illnesses affecting women, such as fast developing cervical cancer; led to the exclusion of women from clinical drug trials and to their having fewer options for treatment than men; and meant that women are often diagnosed late.

3. It does not follow that discredited 'scientific' discoveries will not raise their heads again. It may seem extraordinary, but is nevertheless true, that, in 1991 the old arguments that intelligence is genetically determined and racially linked were raised, in precisely their old form, in articles by Eysenck and Jensen appearing in a special edition of the *Oxford Review of Education.*

CHAPTER TWO

THEMES AND ISSUES

The main foci of this book are political contexts, school change and class-room practice. However, this chapter is concerned with the theoretical understandings which underpin the discussion of anti-racist change and classroom practice later in the book. Although I have, as is conventional, placed it near the beginning of the book, this chapter represents the theoretical positions I have reached as a result of my research. The chapter starts with a discussion of power and social relations and explores ways of thinking about race and racism. Next comes a short section on anti-racist education. For the reasons outlined in the section on 'Theoretical frameworks and everyday life' in the previous chapter, this chapter is the foundation for all that follows.

Power, race and racism

Social relations and discourse

Social relations are organised through a number of institutions and social structures, of which the education system is one (others include the family, the law, the political system, and so on). Within each of these social institutions there are a number of different possible ways of behaving and of understanding the nature of the institution. These different versions of the particular institution are in competition with each other for dominance and, at different times and in different places, different versions will be more or less successful. Indeed, contradictions and conflict are part of the network of social relations with which we all live. If we take the example of education, we can see that the different sides of current struggles around teaching methods (for example, over the use of 'real books' to teach reading) represent a struggle between different understandings of what it means to teach and to learn and different notions of what schooling is for and about.

These competing understandings are expressed through language and through the ways in which institutions like schools are actually organised. The French philosopher, Michel Foucault, used the terms 'discourse' (taken from the field of linguistics) and 'discursive practices' to describe these understandings and their expression through language, organisational forms and ways of behaving.[1] The various discourses which are available in relation to particular social institutions and structures provide us with different possible ways of behaving and understanding the world as well as limiting (but not determining) what can be done and said. We are positioned in various discourses as well as taking up positions ourselves. For example, we identify ourselves and are identified as heterosexual, lesbian or gay and could not do so if categorising discourses of sexuality did not exist. In this limited sense, we can be said to be 'produced' by discourses and discursive practices.

In *Discipline and Punish* (1977), Foucault discusses the ways in which schools have arisen as a site of discipline and surveillance of children, saying that:

> A relation of surveillance, defined and regulated is inscribed at the heart of the practice of teaching, not as an additional or adjacent part, but as a mechanism that is inherent to it and which increases its efficiency.

(p. 176)

Following Foucault, Valerie Walkerdine (1985) argues that discourses in schooling both regulate and produce the child as a 'rational, independent, autonomous [individual] as a quasi- natural phenomenon who progresses through a universalised developmental sequence towards the possibility of rational argument' (p.203). In this context, she suggests that schooling not only 'defines ... what knowledge is, but also defines and regulates what 'a child is' (pp. 207-208). Schools, then, are sites of struggles, not only about knowledge, but also about ideologies of childhood, about what it means to be a teacher and to be gendered. Consequently, there are, within schooling, a number of different, sometimes contradictory, discourses available through which teachers and children are produced and produce themselves.

It is possible, for example, to imagine teachers behaving in a number of different ways in relation to students, and these ways may come from a number of different discourses. The most obvious discourse of teaching might be called the 'instructional discourse'. Within it, teachers pass on information, demonstrate how to do things, and so on. Within this discourse it would be impossible to imagine a teacher knowing less than pupils in her/his class about a topic being taught. However, teachers also operate, especially in the early years of schooling, within what might be called a 'mothering discourse'. In this context, teachers might offer comfort to children who are distressed or look after them in physical ways, such as changing their undergarments if they have 'wet' themselves.[2] It would not, however, be open to a teacher to undertake all the functions of mothering and remain in the role of teacher, and even very young children are aware of the differences in expected behaviours. One little girl, when she was six and a pupil in the school where her mother taught, resolved the conflict of discourses by regularly calling her mother 'Mrs Mummy' when at school.[3] There are, of course, many other discourses within which teachers can and do operate — for example, those of social work, policing and so on.[4]

The question of which discourses are dominant is not a neutral one, for the social meanings given to different discursive practices will vary according to one's position within a particular set of social relations. What seems like common-sense will, in general, represent the interests of dominant groups in society, while what seems 'biased' or 'extreme' may well be those discourses which seek to oppose those interests (although subordinated groups develop their own versions of common-sense). In education, for example, it may seem perfectly reasonable to assume that it is desirable to give a 'balanced' view of controversial and political questions and this is often argued against anti-racist and anti-sexist education. However subjects which are controversial change over time. For example, until relatively recently the teaching of evolutionary theory rather than the creation story as given in Genesis was considered both subversive and controversial. Furthermore, the demands of 'balance' seem rather different depending on one's position in relation to the issue. For example, 'balance' in relation to teaching about South Africa would probably seem very different to Nelson Mandela and to President de Klerk. Equally, it might be salutary to ask oneself what 'balance' might mean in relation to teaching about child sexual abuse.

Questions of power

The concept of power is important in any discussion of social relations. In certain conceptualisations of power, it is reified and written about as if it were something held by certain groups and people and not others. For example, Mullard (1981) writes:

> Neither West Indians, Pakistanis, Indians, nor Africans, nor blacks as a whole, possess anything like the same amounts of power as the white dominant 'British' group. ...
>
> ... Power is held by white groups in society; ... Real power in a capitalist society and ... a racist society is indivisible.
> (p. 130)

Similarly, when Catherine McKinnon (1987) talks of 'the existing *distributions* of power' (p. 141, emphasis added), the implication is that power exists in forms which enable distribution. I would argue that power cannot be and is not distributed in the same way as, for example, slices of cake. Nevertheless, it is important to recognise that power can be and is distributed through the ways in which institutions like schools are organised and tends to accrue to certain groups of people — most obviously white, middle-class, heterosexual men.

11

Foucault argues that power is constructed through 'juridico-political discourse' and other professional discourses (1978, p. 88). He suggests, further, that:

> Power is everywhere; not because it embraces everything, but because it comes from everywhere. ... [P]ower is not an institution, and not a structure; neither is it a certain strength we are endowed with; it is the name that one attributes to a complex strategical situation in a particular society.
>
> (*ibid*, p. 93)

Foucault links power inextricably with knowledge, arguing that power cannot be regarded simply as the operation of repression, law and coercion. He suggests that power works not only in these negative senses but also produces ways of understanding the world (that is, knowledge) and that individuals, their knowledge and identities are also produced through their positioning in discourses and hence through power relations (1977, p. 194).

Foucault's critique of the reification of power is correct. Power is not a 'thing' which exists outside of social relationships. It is constructed and reconstructed in and through them constantly. Neither is it held uniformly by one dominant group in society. One has only to consider the power that a woman can develop in a heterosexual relationship or the position of, for example, a black man and a white woman in relation to each other, to realise that power relationships are more complex than binary notions of either race or gender would suggest.[5]

However, Foucault's position on the construction of power through discourse is also less than satisfactory. He does not offer an adequate account of how discourses come into being or change. Because they exist already and counter (or, as he calls them, 'reverse') discourses always hark back to the dominant, discourses appear to be socially given and transformative resistance to them seems difficult, if not impossible. For example, discourses of gay liberation exist in relation to hexterosexuality and those of anti-racism in relation to racist discourses.

According to Foucault, we are produced as subjects within particular discourses, but he does not pay attention to the ways in which we ourselves produce the discourses in which we are inscribed in certain subject positions — whether they be relatively powerful or powerless. Neither does Foucault offer a full account for the concentration of power in hierarchies, which we can observe in social institutions like schools, nor for the difficulty which people belonging to certain groups (like black women, black men or white women) have in occupying subject positions of power in such institutions. Thus Foucault does not explain adequately the role that institutional structures have in maintaining power relations (see, also, Hall 1988).

In using the concept of power I would, therefore, wish to pay attention to the complexity of power relationships raised by Foucault's discussion of discourses. I would wish particularly to note that power is not always wielded through coercion, but often through discursive practices which people, as active agents within these practices, either consent to or resist. It is, however, not always clear what constitutes consent or resistance. For example, academic success on the part of young black women in schools may appear to be consent to discourses of school, but can also be conceived of as resistance to discourses which place black students as 'underachievers'.

Neither should we forget that power is also often wielded through the forces of coercion (for example, by the police and the weight of institutional hierarchies). It is important to hold on to notions of material existence, a kind of 'reality' which imposes itself on people, in order to avoid falling into relativism. It is more difficult for some people to occupy powerful positions than others. This is due not just to discourse but to the material realities through which the dice are loaded against some. For example, it is more difficult for a white woman, a black woman or black man to become a head of a school than it is for a white man.

It is also important to note that we may occupy positions within different and contradictory discourses, being, at one and the same time, in positions of relative power and relative powerlessness. For example, an anti-racist teacher in a state school will be relatively powerful in relation to her/his pupils, but relatively powerless in relation to people such as inspectors, the head of the school or local councillors, especially if the latter are supportive of dominant, racist discourses. The way this sometimes works will be illustrated in case studies presented later in the book.

Race and racist discourses

There are a number of discourses around issues of race and racism in education and other social structures. One of our most widespread common-sense understandings is that 'race' exists as an objective social fact. We categorise ourselves and others by their notional race (and/or colour) with hardly a thought as to the origin of these categories. It is instructive to consider where these notions come from, for without the notion that people can be categorised according to supposedly 'objective' characteristics, it would not be possible to think in terms of 'race'. If this were the case, then racist discourses, as we understand them, would be impossible (although discrimination and oppression on other grounds than 'race', as we understand it, could/would still exist).

It is now widely accepted that notions of race are socially constructed, with biological variations between people of the same 'race' being as wide as, or wider than, variations between people of notionally different 'races'. As Rose et al. (1984) point out:

> ... it turns out not to matter much how the groups are assigned [to particular races], because the differences between major 'racial' categories, no matter how defined, turn out to be small. Human 'racial'

13

differentiation is, indeed, only skin deep. Any use of racial categories must take its justifications from some other source than biology. (pp.126-7)

Nevertheless, 'race' continues to be a major category through which we understand the world. For most social scientists, the assumption is that what needs to be explained is the existence of racism, and that it is prejudice and discrimination which is the primary problem. However, I would argue that what we need to explain is the existence of the concept of 'race' in the first place.

The concept of 'race'

Science and rationalism are dominant discourses in Western intellectual thought. When we seek answers to questions which puzzle us, we invariably turn to 'science' for the answers. One of the characteristics of Western science is that it categorises, and the post-Darwinian assumption has been that people can be categorised in similar ways to chemical elements, plants, animals and so forth.

In the process of categorisation, it has been assumed that particular groups of people have certain essential[6] characteristics, which are (usually) biologically determined. Thus, for example, in certain racist discourses African-Caribbean men and women are assumed to be naturally 'physical', while South Asian women are assumed to be naturally 'passive'. It has been further assumed that when someone has been categorised, or has categorised him or herself, according to one of a number of types of categories, which include race, gender, sexuality, ability and so on, then everything important which can be said about this person has, in fact, been said. In this way, social identities such as those of race are constructed. Such social identities are not simply about how we are seen or categorised. They are also important in how we ourselves experience and understand the world.

In terms of race, it is assumed, in keeping with the essentialist processes of categorisation discussed above, that certain kinds of people are 'black' and other kinds of people are 'white'. This is the basis of racism directed against black people. The concepts *race* and *racism* are mutually dependent. This is not a static situation, but a dynamic process in which racist discourses feed on the concept of race, and in which the concept of race is constantly re-articulated and reproduced through racist discourses in a symbiotic relationship.

What is racism?

I would suggest that racism can be best understood in terms of process — or, perhaps, those processes which result in disadvantage for particular groups of people defined through racist discourses. In this society and historical context the people against whom racist processes work are most often black, but, at other times and in other places, other groups, such as the

Irish or Jews, have been the chief butt of different forms of racism and it should be noted that anti-Irish racism in Britain and anti-semitism more generally continue to be active and, indeed, seem to be on the increase.

Because racism is a process, which changes over time and place and varies with macro- and micro-political conditions, it is not possible to give a simple, straightforward definition to the word. Racism cannot be reduced to a simple formula, such as the often quoted equation 'racism equals power plus prejudice'. Certainly both prejudice and power play a part in the construction of racism (or, since it takes many forms, racisms). However, as can be seen from the discussion above, power is more complicated than such a formula allows for and personal prejudice is not necessarily a component in every situation in which black people are disadvantaged. If, for example, an oversubscribed school offers places first to those children who have had a sibling there (even if the sibling has left), which is very common, this is likely to disadvantage black children in areas where there have been relatively recent influxes of black people. It is unlikely that such a practice would have originated from the prejudiced intention of reducing the numbers of black pupils, but this will be the effect. It is practices such as these which are defined as 'indirect racism' in the Race Relations Act 1976. The operation of the 'market' in education under the Education Reform Act (ERA) will also disadvantage black pupils disproportionately. However it was instituted at the behest of New Right economic ideology rather than directly by racism.

Racism involves a variety of processes and institutional arrangements which are socially constructed. These processes take place both at macro-levels, involving national and even global politics, and at micro-levels, in the organisation of particular institutions like schools and in the relationships between individuals.

As pointed out above, one of the processes involved in the construction of racism is the acceptance, as common-sense, of racial categories. However, racism cannot be combated simply by refusing to accept racial categories. The adoption of slogans such as 'One race the human race', while it may be an important aim, does not recognise that racism makes a real difference in the material world to people's life chances and experiences (Henriques 1984) and may even be a form of racism itself in its refusal to recognise difference.

Explanations of racism offered by the various social sciences over the last twenty years have tended to concentrate on either personal racism and the psychology of prejudice or on institutional racism and the racist structures of society. All such theorisations have assumed a split between the individual and society. However, I would wish to follow Henriques et al. (1984) in suggesting that this is a false dichotomy, for the individuals cannot exist outside of society and society is composed of individuals and groups of individuals. This individual-society dualism, as Henriques says, 'allows even radical analyses to be pressed into the service of existing social relations, thereby reinforcing and perpetuating them' for if everything is determined by the structure of society, there is little possibility for change

(p. 60). Henriques points out that the liberal notion of prejudice as individual responsibility and the radical idea that responsibility lies with 'the system' are locked together, one on each side of the individual-society dichotomy, 'in a mutually propelling antagonism' (p. 62).

Henriques et al. (op cit) begin to develop explanations of relations of both race and gender through the development of an analysis which draws on Foucauldian ideas about discourse, on psychoanalysis, and understandings of socio-economic and political factors. In doing so, they point out that none of these factors operates on its own or can be said the be the primary cause of racism or sexism.

It is important to recognise that the operation of racism is both complex and differentiated, particularly in the context of attempts to combat it. There are, as stated above, many racisms, not just one. What they have in common is the outcome of black disadvantage in housing, employment, education, and many other areas of everyday life.[7] It should, however, be noted that while conferring advantage on white people, racism overlays anxiety and fear. This can be clearly seen in events such as the beating of Rodney King by police in Los Angeles in March 1991 because, in the words of the police officers, they were 'terrified' of his 'superhuman strength' and that 'if he got up ... he would grab my gun and shoot me' — all this in spite of the fact that King was being beaten senseless and was surrounded by six police officers all with guns, batons and 'stun-guns' (*Newsnight,* BBC2, April 30 1992). Even if these statements by the police were simply excuses invented at the time of their trial, the fact that they led to the acquittal of the officers in the face of overwhelming video evidence shows that such fear and anxiety had currency amongst the white jurors. This fear and anxiety is perpetuated by racism so that the process is circular (see, also, Fanon 1986, Bhabha in his introduction to Fanon and 1983, 1986).

Identity and politics

Essentialism and oppositional politics

The assumption, discussed above, that people's identities are determined by biological factors is one which has been powerful not only in dominant ideologies of, for example, racism, but also in oppositional ideologies and discourses. This can be seen in the development of a series of slogans by different oppositional groups such as 'Black is beautiful', 'Sisterhood is powerful' and 'Gay is good'. All these slogans privilege one characteristic of a person over all others — be it race/colour, gender or sexuality. The common underlying assumption is that the single most important characteristic of a person is the one acknowledged in the slogan and, implicitly, that 'being black/female/gay' describes the essence or 'real' core of one's being.

Such assumptions have been questioned in a variety of ways, most importantly for the way in which the blanket inclusion of everybody in a particular group as being 'essentially' the same is an erasure of difference which actually marginalises the experience of some people in that category. Thus, for example, black women have challenged assumptions by white feminists that the experience of all women is of a kind (see, for example, Carby 1982, Parmar 1982) and black lesbians have challenged both sexism and homophobia within black communities (see, for example, Gomez and Smith 1990). Yet others have raised issues of class and disability. It is clear, then, that the ways in which racism is experienced and the effects that it has on black people will vary according to their positioning within both racist discourses and others, such as those of class, gender and sexuality.

Nevertheless, essentialising slogans have played a necessary part in the construction of positive identities by people in subordinated groups and the development of oppositional strategies has often rested on these identities. People in subordinated groups may well find that essentialist ideas about identity are necessary constructions if they are to establish the solidarity of recognised common experience in order to fight their oppression. Essentialism is thus part of a strategy of resistance and is necessary in certain political moments, such as in the development of Black Consciousness in the context of the struggle for Civil Rights in the United States in the 1960s and in South Africa in the 1970s (see, for example, Biko 1978).

Furthermore people (especially those in marginalised groups) are nearly always treated by others as having essential identities related to their race, sexuality, gender or some other characteristic. Racism, for example, is a form of essentialist politics, whether it is based on biological notions of white superiority or on notions of the cultural superiority of Western society, as in recent versions of what has been labelled the 'New Racism' (Barker 1981). In the hands of those in dominant groups, essentialist politics are always reactionary. However, as pointed out above, in the hands of subordinated groups, such politics may, at certain historical moments, be progressive.

The problem is that oppositional forms of politics based on essentialist notions of identity are both necessary and dangerous: necessary in the construction of opposition to dominant, oppressive ideologies; dangerous in that they are, inevitably, locked into the dominant discourses which categorise people (according to race, gender, sexuality, class, ability, and so on) and, for this reason, feed these dominant discourses. They are also dangerous because the other side of the coin which claims that all members of a group are the same (for example, in the category woman or black) is an ever-increasing fragmentation (with smaller and smaller groups proclaiming their identities).

So, on the one hand, the erasure of difference is likely to marginalise some people, while, on the other, non-recognition of commonality of experience could lead to a situation in which political action becomes almost impossible. For example, definitions of the category 'black' as including Africans,

17

Caribbeans, South Asians and sometimes other groups who experience discrimination, such as Turkish or Greek Cypriots, have been criticised because they ignore the differences between the experiences of colonisation and immigration of these different groups. On the other hand, the search for an unambiguous lesbian and gay identity[8] has, on occasion, led to the questioning of the right of certain people to define themselves as lesbian or gay, with the result that considerable time and vituperation has been expended in trying to establish who is 'really' entitled to be at a closed lesbian and gay meeting — at the expense of developing strategies for opposing lesbian and gay oppression.

Subjectivity and identity

The development of subjective identities is both complex and important, and identities themselves are multi- faceted and contradictory. They are formed through a combination of available discourses, personal experience and material existence. Psychoanalysis has a major contribution to make to our understanding of this, since it explores subjectivity and the importance of the unconscious construction of the 'Other' in the formation of identity. All the major social binary opposites (white/black, heterosexual/homosexual, male/female, bourgeois/working class, etc) rely, in the construction of subjective identities, on 'othering' those on the other side of the divide. It is by drawing boundaries and placing others outside those boundaries that we establish our identities.

People have major emotional, often unconscious commitments to these identities which are usually defined with reference to groups 'other' than the one identified with. Indeed, it is difficult to see how categories of social identity could exist without reference to some other, and different, category. We are women because we are not men, black because we are not white and so on. Furthermore, the categories are not only those of difference. They are established in hierarchical ways, so that one category is dominant. From our earliest experiences in a racist and sexist society, we are invited to identify ourselves in these ways in relation to the opposite gender and/or race.

Thus, as the various categories of 'kinds of people' are produced, so too are others, which are seen as opposite, the other side of a binary divide. The group categories on either side of the divide are seen to be mutually exclusive and, usually, hostile to each other. 'Us' is not only different to 'them'. 'They' are also (often/usually) 'our' enemies. Indeed, it is not only people who are placed in opposing categories. It is also 'common-sense' to suppose that, for example, 'mind' and 'body' are binary opposites. This process can be seen at a number of different levels of understanding. 'Individual' and 'society' are understood to be binary opposites, as well as 'black' and 'white', 'men' and 'women', 'heterosexual' and 'homosexual', and so on. It should be noted here that disgust and desire are intimately linked; love and hate as opposite sides of the same coin. Thus images of black people are infused with images of sexuality (Fanon 1986, Bhabha in his introduction to Fanon); Africa is portrayed as both savage and a sexual woman in Victorian novels such as those by Rider Haggard and Joseph Conrad; and the myth of black men as rapists of white women persists (Davis 1982, hooks 1982). A recent example of the attraction for the 'Other' was the announcement that the son of President de Klerk of South Africa was to marry a black woman.

Racist discourses which demonise black people as the (monstrous) 'Other' in, for example, popular media (but also in school books and children's fiction — see, for example, Klein 1985 and 1986) go some way towards the production of racism. However, at the same time (and, indeed, in the same moment) as mass media and various politicians[9] construe black people as 'them' and white people as 'us', an alternative and oppositional 'them' and 'us' are constructed in which the 'us' consists of black people (and, sometimes, white anti-racists) and the 'them' of white people.[10]

It is important to realise that the construction of 'thems' and 'us-es' is not something which is done to people simply through mechanisms such as 'socialisation', which imply the individual- society dichotomy challenged above. People are active agents in the making of their own meanings and identities, but, in doing so, they can only use the discourses and material conditions available to them, and these will vary across time and place.

It is also important to realise that, because we have investments in our identities, we also have investments in the differences and inequalities by which we are produced and which we ourselves produce. The types of investments we have in particular discourses of inequality will, of course, vary according to our positions within them. The social and psychic investments of white people in racist discourses are, perhaps, obvious — though it should be noted that white people are not necessarily personally guilty for racism since they are not individually responsible for already existing racist structures and discourses.

Nevertheless, the advantages which accrue from being positioned as white within such discourses cannot be escaped by dint of being an active anti-racist. This is at its most obvious in South Africa, where even political activists imprisoned for their opposition to apartheid are treated differentially according to their skin colour. However it is also true in Britain and other Western countries, where the contrasts of position are not usually as stark as in South Africa, that white people are more likely than black people to occupy positions of power, both materially and subjectively. For example, the annual Department of Employment Gazette shows clearly that Caribbean and South Asian people are more likely than white people to be unemployed and, when employed are more likely to hold jobs for which they are 'over-qualified'.

The psychic and social investments of black people in racist discourses are considerably less obvious. However, the very act of identifying as 'black' is (as pointed out above) both a positive source of resistance and subversion of dominant racist ideologies and, at the same time, dependent on the very racist discourses which produce skin colour of those constructed as 'black' and other characteristics associated with 'blackness' as being of overriding importance.

Just as white people take up positions in multiple and often contradictory discourses, so too do black people. They may, for example, find it politically and emotionally necessary both to affirm their black identities and to question the whole concept of race, on which such identities depend. Equally, they may have institutionally powerful positions and be subjected on a daily basis to racism. For example, the relatively few black school inspectors may experience racism emanating from those in institutionally less powerful positions than themselves.

The questions raised by this complexity are those of how racism is produced and reproduced and how strategies for change can be developed. In order to combat racism, we need an account which recognises historical, political and locational specificities and which grapples with the intransigence of the psychic and social investments which people have in the *status quo*. Racist discourses both produce, and are produced by, the subjectivities of white and black people and the practices involved in these discourses constitute and are constituted by the power relations and institutional arrangements of racism.

What I have tried to do in this book is to maintain an awareness of the complexity of the subject throughout, while developing practical approaches in the classroom through which children and teachers can be involved in the deconstruction of racist ideologies and discourses and the reconstruction of anti-racist ones.

Anti-racist education

In the early 1980s there was considerable debate between those who proposed curriculum change such that children would meet a variety of 'cultures' in the course of their schooling and those who proposed change aimed at countering racism. For example, the Rampton Report argued that:

> A 'good' education cannot be based on one culture only, and in Britain where ethnic minorities form a permanent and integral part of the population, we do not believe that education should seek to iron out the differences between cultures, nor attempt to draw everyone into the dominant culture. On the contrary, it will draw upon the experiences of the many cultures that make up our society and thus broaden the cultural horizons of every child. That is what we mean by 'multicultural' education.

> (Committee of Inquiry into the Education of Children from Ethnic Minority Groups 1981, p. 27)

Such views were criticised by protagonists of anti-racist education, who claimed that multiculturalists failed to show evidence of any improvement in either academic achievement of black children or equality of opportunity (see, for example, Troyna 1983, p.425). Others argued that multicultural education was, in Madeleine Arnot's words 'addressing the wrong audience, tackling the wrong problem and doing it in the wrong way (i.e. through curriculum development' (1986, p.32). Arnot characterised anti-racism in the following way:

(a) It recognised the importance of locating the education system and education policy in the broader political and economic context of race relations. Labour market inequality is understood not as a symptom of black disadvantage but as the manifestation of the power relations between black and white people in the UK ...

(b) Anti-racist education policy would wish to deal explicitly with race and racism in education and training. Racial prejudice and stereotypes constitute the reality that undermines black pupils' identities and their sense of personal value. It also shapes the way they are treated in education and in the labour market. The aim, therefore, ...should be to tackle *white racism* in all schools irrespective of their cultural mix'.

(ibid pp 33-34, emphasis in original).

This debate was politically important at the time, since it established that the 'problem' for education was racism, not the existence of cultural diversity. The debate continues to have certain resonance and is of theoretical importance. My own understanding of anti-racist education is that it should form part 'of a more broadly conceived programme of political education' (Carrington and Troyna 1988, p. 208); should embrace both policy and practice; should aim at removing structural inequalities; and should be directed towards enabling young people (and adults) to challenge dominant ideologies and develop counter discourses. In so doing, as will become clear in the case studies of classroom practice in chapter 7, it is necessary to democratise classrooms and develop collaborative learning in ways which 'enhance the cognitive, social and affective development of children' (Carrington and Short 1989, p.21).

This is a matter as much for processes of teaching and learning as it is for curriculum content. While the National Curriculum sets out most of the content of the curriculum, classroom processes continue to be within the control of teachers — although current political educational debates about teaching methods may threaten this. The rest of this book is concerned with possibilities for change in schools given national and local political contexts and the specifics of individual schools and classrooms.

References for Chapter 2

1. For further accessible explanation of the term 'discourse', see Weedon (1987). Foucault's own use of the term is exemplified in many publications, but perhaps most accessibly in *The History of Sexuality, Vol. 1* (1978), *Discipline and Punish* (1977) and in Rabinow (ed) *The Foucault Reader* (1984).

2. It is, of course, the case that both male and female teachers can and do operate within discourse of mothering.

3. See Burgess and Carter (1992a and forthcoming) for an elaboration of mothering discourses in primary schooling.

4. Child-centredness is an important discourse, particularly in primary education. See chapter 6 for further discussion of this.

5. Throughout this text, I have used the word 'black' to indicate those groups discriminated against on the grounds of their skin colour and certain other associated physical and cultural characteristics, and 'white' to indicate 'not black'. However, it is important to recognise that this usage, which was developed in the 1980s as a way of making a political statement about the experience of racism, is increasingly being questioned by those who prefer to define themselves in terms of 'ethnicity'. Consequently, it is now common to see the usages 'black and Asian' or 'African-Caribbean and Asian'. I have chosen to continue with the use of 'black' partly for the sake of brevity but, more importantly, because I believe that the political point about racism remains valid.

6. I have used the term 'essential' to indicate both 'something at the core, of the essence' and 'necessary'.

7. For examples of such discrimination see, *inter alia,* Epstein and Sealey (1990), C.R.E. (1988a, 1988b, 1988c) Kelly and Cohn, (1988), Siraj-Blatchford (1991).

8. The question here is, 'what makes a person lesbian or gay?' Lesbianism, for example, has been defined by Adrienne Rich (1983) to include all women who are, in any way, 'woman-identified', whilst others have insisted that it is the sex act with another woman which constitutes lesbianism.

9. For example, Norman Tebbitt's (in)famous 'cricket test' by which 'we' (white people) will know whether 'they' (black people) are truly British is an example of the process of constructing people as 'other'. In this example black people are positioned as 'unpatriotic', 'disloyal' and a host of other epithets which would indicate their lack of 'Britishness'.

10. A similar process can be seen at work in the production of lesbian and gay identities, and, in particular, of the way in which the introduction of Section 28 of the Local Government Act 1988 had the unintended result of itself 'promoting homosexuality' (see Stacey 1991).

CHAPTER THREE

THE NEW RIGHT

This chapter is concerned with the impact of national and local politics on the possibilities and likelihood of anti-racist change in education. Schools and local education authorities are not islands, floating in a vacuum. National politics have a considerable impact on the negotiations which take place within schools (Ball 1987, pp. 260-278) and on the ease with which change can be achieved.

The purpose of this chapter, then, is not to analyse the National Curriculum in detail. Neither is it my intention to give detailed attention to an analysis of the writings of the New Right in the *Black Papers* and elsewhere (e.g. Palmer 1986).[1] Rather, I am concerned to examine the impact on teachers — and, consequently, on possibilities for change — of these ideas and of other aspects of national politics. New Right thinking will, therefore, be analysed just enough to provide a basis for understanding its effect on the development of anti-racist education.

Lack of social recognition of teachers has contributed to a demoralisation which makes the risk-taking involved in developing anti-racist education an unattractive option. However, I would also suggest that an unwillingness on the part of teachers to be accountable to students and parents has made it easier for the New Right to find support for attacking teachers and other public professionals and that this has had implications for possibilities of 'selling' anti-racism in education.

In spite of the dominance of 'anti-anti-racist' discourses in the popular media, there have been counter-discourses in national politics, as evidenced by the publication of the Rampton (Committee of Inquiry into the Education of Children from Ethnic Minority Groups 1981) and Swann (Committee of Inquiry into the Education of Children from Ethnic Minority Groups 1985) Reports. I will suggest that these counter-discourses made the development of anti-racist education a possibility, even though the general climate was unfavourable. I will argue further that, despite the general deprioritisation of equality issues in the light of demands made on teachers and the ERA, there are still possibilities for such developments.

The New Right on race and education

Dale (1989, pp 80-89) suggests that there are several separate strands in Thatcher's Conservative Party: the pragmatic 'industrial trainers'; the traditional and paternalistic 'Old Tories'; the 'populists', appealing 'to unifying' factors like nationality above 'divisive' factors like class, race and gender; the 'moral entrepreneurs' who 'see education at the heart of a fight for a particular morality and against (im)moralities which would undermine it' (p. 85); and the 'privatizers', who adhere to neo-liberal philosophies about individualism and the market. However by 1988, Dale suggests, 'the cornerstone of the new settlement [was] the market' (p. 116).

In this he is at one with Ball (1990a and 1990b), who suggests that the neo-liberal ideas of Hayek form the philosophical basis of the ERA. Ball argues that the education market was established by the ERA through the enshrinement of parental choice, competition in schools, diversity of provision and devolution of funding (Local Management):

> The model of organization which the ERA implies is clear, it is that of governors as Board of Directors and head teacher as Chief Executive. Schools are to become businesses, run and managed like businesses with a primary focus on the profit and loss account. The parent is now the customer, the pupils in effect the product. Those schools which produce shoddy goods, it is believed will lose custom. And it would appear that in the government's view shoddy goods mean 'poor' results in national tests. ... Given that schools are also required to provide a fixed National Curriculum it is tempting to refine the business model slightly and see the education market as a system of franchises, what one writer has called 'Kentucky Fried Schooling' (Hargreaves, 1989)

> (Ball 1990a, p.11)

Both Dale and Ball argue that the likely outcome of ERA will be the further development of inequality between favoured schools in the leafy suburbs and under-resourced schools in the inner cities. However neither of them discusses the specific impact this will have on 'racial' inequality, nor do they mention the role that anti-anti-racism has played in the development, popularisation and implementation of New Right ideas about education.

Jones (1989), distinguishing between Conservative modernisers and traditionalists, describes Conservative education policy as 'Janus-headed, fus[ing] the archaic and the modern, mix[ing] nostalgia with technology, evok[ing] community and promot[ing] entrepreneurialism' (p.1). He sees the 'Conservative revolution' as characterised by tensions between these different tendencies, which combine for 'one common purpose: to eliminate the major tendencies that have dominated post-war education policy, and to replace them with a quite different order of priorities' (ibid, p.1).

Jones points out the importance that replacing the discourse of equal opportunities and egalitarianism with one of quality and standards has assumed in Tory rhetoric.[2] In this regard, he points particularly to the role of anti-anti-racism both in popularising Tory policies and marginalising their opponents:

> Labour could be presented as the mere defender of minority causes, which had no purchase on the major issues of the educational agenda. Where these causes were not irrelevant, they were positively malign in their effects on family life and cultural cohesion. In this attack on 'loony leftism', ministers increasingly drew their weapons from the armoury of right-wing thought: the ideas of culture and nation developed on the right became central to the offensive against Labour in local government. Race and sexuality became front-line political issues.
>
> (*ibid*, p. 27)

Jones goes on to point out that racism has played a crucial part in the development of New Right ideas about education, particularly in the hands of Scruton and Honeyford — two of the most effective and influential thinkers about education on the New Right — whose ideas he effectively demolishes (*ibid*, pp. 52-64). He suggests that, notwithstanding the intellectual poverty of their ideas, they have appealed to a popular racism which has provided part of the appeal of ERA to many parents. For example, both opting out and open enrolment provide the opportunity for white parents to keep their children away from schools with large numbers of black pupils — and in 1987 'an opinion poll conducted for London Weekend Television found that more than 40% of white parents in the south-east favoured race-segregated schools' (ibid, p. 6). Jones' prediction has subsequently been confirmed, and, in October 1991 a court ruling established that the ERA takes precedence over the Race Relations Act.[3]

Furthermore, the National Curriculum, as Johnson (1991a) says, is partly an attempt to produce a sense of national British/English identity which:

> implements years of campaigning around 'sociology' and 'social science', peace studies, sex education, religious instruction, anti-racist and multicultural education and around 'progressive education' and 'second-order subjects' more generally. It is the culmination of the Black Paper campaigns, many themes of which were revived in the formative period of 1985-7. Like these campaigns, the curriculum favours conventional subject categories to exclude what it disapproves of. It imposes its 'standards' negatively; it stops the rot.
>
> (p. 70)

One characteristic, then, of New Right thinking has been the development of what has come to be know as 'anti-anti-racism'. In this discourse, anti-racism is seen as a major threat (in Palmer's (1986) words, an 'assault') to the social and moral order of society. In terms of the different strands of

New Right thinking, anti-anti-racism has a place in both neo-conservative and neo-liberal aspects. For the neo-conservatives, anti-racism represents a threat to national identity and traditional values, particularly in its incorporation of 'alien cultures'. For the neo-liberals there is a denial of racism as a cause of inequality. Their radical individualism indicates that the 'achievement' of black people is a function of individual effort and virtue and they draw attention to the success of some black businessmen[4] as an indication that the market is open to all to enter in the same way.

Ball (1990b) has tellingly labelled the discourses, begun in the *Black Papers* in the 1970s and continued through the public campaign of the 1980s, 'the discourses of derision' (pp. 31-42). In these discourses, as Ball comments:

> The social-subject of neo-conservatism is the loyal, law-abiding family man (or housewife/mother), holder of and believer in traditional values and sober virtues. Over and against this ideal citizen/parent is set an alternative subject: the carrier of alien values or alien culture, the agitator/trade unionist, sexual deviant, or working, single-parent mother, permissive/liberal, and progressive teacher — in other words 'the enemy within', the traitor.
>
> (Ball 1990b, p. 40)

The position of teachers in relation to the 'discourses of derision' has been complex and contradictory. On the one hand, they are held to be the cause of many of the nations' ills, while on the other, they are themselves summoned to be 'upright citizens' in the way Ball describes above. In this respect, it should not be forgotten that, according to a poll carried out by the *Times Educational Supplement (TES)*, the majority of teachers voted Conservative in the 1979 election (cited in Johnson 1991a, p. 44).[5]

Although Johnson (1991b) discusses his own grappling with the ideas of the New Right and, to some extent, its impact on his own work as a university lecturer, none of the authors mentioned above discusses the ways in which New Right thinking — apart from nationally imposed policy — has had an impact directly on teachers and in schools. My question is, 'How have discourses changed *in* schools in response to the New Right?'

Most teachers, like other members of the general public, have not actually read the *Black Papers, the Salisbury Review* or books like Palmer's (1986) *Anti-racism — an assault on education and value*. However, from 1986 through to the present, writers of the New Right have had regular columns in the *TES*.[6] This paper is taken by a large number of teachers and in a large number of schools up and down the country. While looking at job advertisements, teachers also read the paper and become involved in discussions about articles in it. New Right columnists have used their columns to argue for their educational politics over a range of issues from the teaching of reading to the role of the teacher, and, of course, have commented frequently and vehemently on the evils of anti-racism in education.[7] Teachers do read these columns, though I believe that their direct influence is small. Nevertheless, their very appearance on a regular basis has drawn the centre of gravity of arguments about education to the right.

What I believe has been more influential has been the more insidious, because unsigned and apparently 'neutral', influence of the television news and current affairs programmes and the shift to the right of the traditionally 'liberal' *Guardian,* both in its editorial policy on education and in signed articles. In September 1986, for example, the *Guardian* carried an article on Brent's race policies and the National Union of Teachers (NUT). This article was highly critical of Brent, not on the grounds of ineffectiveness or the imposition of equal opportunities policies without adequate consultation, but simply on the grounds of appointing '180 race inspectors'. While spokespeople from the Brent NUT were extensively quoted in the article, the voices of those supporting the policy and the establishment of the Development Programme for Race Equality were notably absent (*Guardian* 11.9.86).

Of course, the columns in the *TES* and the *Guardian* formed only a minor sub-plot in a much wider and more general campaign against anti-racism, which found expression in the columns of the tabloid press, television coverage, speeches by politicians and government policies. An important part of this campaign, was the recruitment of (anti-)heroes and heroines to the ranks of the New Right. People such as Maureen McGoldrick in Brent, Philip Savery in Avon and Ray Honeyford in Bradford were incorporated into the pantheon of martyrs in the cause of 'freedom'.

The Honeyford affair played a particularly important role in the campaign against anti-racism. For example, near the beginning of the campaign against Brent, the *Daily Mail* published a full-page version of Honeyford's *Spectator* article (*Daily Mail* 12.9.86). In this article, Honeyford wrote about the way in which, he said, racist name-calling was used by children in his school as a mark of friendship and trust and, from this, drew the conclusion that anti-racists were wrong to find such derogatory language offensive. It is, of course, true that many people in marginalised groups use such language to describe themselves — it is, for example, common for lesbians to describe themselves as 'dykes' and the use of the term 'nigger' has, on occasion, been adopted by African Americans — partly as a conscious attempt to reclaim the language. This does not make these words any less offensive when used by those in dominant groups in the ways described by Honeyford.

What is particularly interesting about the Honeyford affair was the way in which he was swiftly adopted both as a 'folk-hero' of the New Right and popular press and invited to join the ranks of those with direct influence on government, being invited, for example, to Downing Street to discuss education policy with the Prime Minister. Not only was he adopted in the popular media, but his name rapidly became a by-word in schools, a code for discrediting anti-racist education. In this respect, it is interesting to note that in 1991, a teacher in a middle school in Warwickshire reported to me that, in his school, the Honeyford affair was still widely referred to in discussions about anti-racist and multicultural education.[8]

Attacks on Brent

Attacks on the London Borough of Brent during the summer and autumn of 1986 formed an important part of the campaign against anti-racist and multicultural education. In representing Brent as wicked, divisive and dictatorial and associating its anti-racist policies with the 'loony left' of the Labour Party, the media cleared a way for the issue of race to be a theme of the 1987 general election. While there were undoubtedly many actions taken by Brent LEA which were mistaken and even counter-productive — often resting on bureaucratic mechanisms and open to charges of authoritarianism — it remains the case that the negative image of Brent and other left Labour authorities was largely constructed out of exaggeration and fabrication (Gordon 1990, p. 189).

This campaign around Brent's policies and programme had the effect of legitimising attacks on anti-racist education, and subsequently the press used the 'race spies' slander as a short-hand way of attacking anti-racist education. In schools it became more difficult to raise questions about racism, because many teachers would dismiss them with statements like 'We don't want to be like Brent'. The impact was both immediate and long-lived.

Anti-racism and anti-heterosexism

Concurrently with the campaign against Brent, the media were also attacking the London Borough of Haringey, both for its anti-racist and its anti-heterosexist policies. The popular press had previously focused on the uprising on the Broadwater Farm estate, representing black people as crazed rioters (Gifford 1986 and 1988), but during 1986-88 were more concerned with stories of a 'crusade for [homosexuality], by having it taught in schools and written about in books for children as something quite admirable' (*Today* 2.9.86). However:

> To understand more fully the conflict over Haringey's lesbian and gay rights policy it needs to be placed within the context of Haringey's recent history. We need to return to the autumn of 1985 when a council estate in Haringey, pushed to its limit by economic deprivation, racism and police harassment fought back. State agencies responded by occupying Broadwater Farm and restricting the activities of its residents, in a manner which showed a total disregard for the rights of Black and [other] working-class people of their environment. ... The media echoed their own outrage as press reports became increasingly distended, but it did not concern police treatment of parental rights to be informed of their children's arrest. Instead they focused their attack on the council and its leader, Bernie Grant, and condemned Haringey's anti-racist policies. (Cooper 1989, p. 47)

28

Homophobia and heterosexism are more widely considered to be acceptable behaviours than is racism. Thus, by associating anti-racism with anti-hetero-sexism, the tabloid press, in particular, found it easier to discredit anti-racism.

This should not be taken to indicate that homophobia and heterosexism should not be opposed. Nor should it be taken to indicate that there should not be an integrated challenge to different forms of social inequality. The problem is with the way in which the Right make the associations, and the motivation behind them, rather than with the associations in and of them-selves. In this respect, it is similar to the appropriation by the right of what were originally oppositional discourses in other areas[9] and is not a particu-larly new phenomenon. Gramsci (1971, pp. 105-120), in his *Prison Note-books* (written in the early 1930s), pointed to the way in which radical social change could be carried out by the Right in ways which both included and limited programmes which had historically originated on the left.

Like events in Brent, those in Haringey need to be seen in the context of the Conservative Party's campaign for the local elections in London in May 1986 and the general election of June 1987. This particular media campaign seemed designed to split off black groups from other oppositional groups, and, in particular, lesbian and gay groups and the Labour left. Thus, during autumn 1986 the Parents' Rights Group, which had been set up to oppose Haringey Council's policies on lesbian and gay equality, began to emphasise that they spoke on behalf of Haringey's ethnic minorities and, especially, parents who were members of black churches and religious leaders. In this attempt, they were only partially successful, though many black people did see the Council's policies on lesbian and gay equality as an attempt to divert attention from racism (Cooper 1989, pp 55-56).

However such success as they had was not confined to Haringey. For example, one senior teacher involved in anti-racist education in another Authority went out of her way to dissociate her LEA's anti-racist policies from policies on lesbian and gay rights, saying 'We don't want to have anything to do with lesbian and gay rights policies. It's racism of the worst kind to associate black people with those perverts'.

One of the reasons for this partial success is, of course, that black heterosexuals are just as likely to be homophobic as white — just as white lesbians and gays are as likely to be racist as white heterosexuals (see also Epstein, forthcoming). Thus splitting the two groups off from each other is eased. As bell hooks (1989) says:

> Often black gay folk feel extremely isolated because there are tensions in their relationships with the larger, predominately white gay com-munity created by racism, and tensions within black communities around issues of homophobia.

(p.130)

29

Similarly, *Black Out,* one of a series of programmes on BBC2 called *The Black Bag* (broadcast in March 1991), drew attention both to homophobia within the black communities and the racism experienced by black lesbians and gays.

The attacks on lesbian and gay rights policies were in some ways even more effective in shifting the debate to the right in schools than were similar attacks on anti-racist policies. This was partly because of the difficulty for lesbian and gay teachers, parents and students in being 'out' at school, which meant that most teachers did not know anyone who was openly lesbian or gay. It was also because, while anti-racism was, at least, on the agenda of such mainstream organisations as the National Union of Teachers (if not very effectively), anti-heterosexism was not.

There were no major debates at NUT Conferences about lesbian and gay equality until 1988, the year in which Section 28 of the Local Government Act outlawed 'promoting homosexuality' by local authorities. Guidelines on lesbian and gay issues for teachers were not produced by the NUT until February 1991, while preliminary guidelines on racism were produced as early as 1978. National and local courses to train NUT representatives in issues of race in education were held by the NUT from the early 1980s onwards, while there have, as yet, been no equivalent courses on lesbian and gay issues. This does not, of course, mean that the NUT has been effective, or even whole-hearted, in opposing racism. However, it is an indication of the mainstream agenda of teachers and Union officials in the NUT. Similarly AMMA (Assistant Masters and Mistresses Association) has guidelines for anti-racist/multicultural education but has still not addressed lesbian and gay inequalities in education.

This relative failure to adopt anti-heterosexist policies, has not prevented the New Right from making strenuous efforts to associate anti-racism with anti-heterosexism:

> ... there is nothing to stop us from rivalling this demand by inventing a new 'antism'. Why not an anti-handist, anti-hairist, anti-dressist — or even anti-wardenist — curriculum? Since it has recently been argued that education should combat the rampant 'heterosexism' of the school curriculum — because it does not actively and explicitly challenge prejudice against homosexuals — it should not surprise us if already existing courses of anti-racist mathematics are soon augmented by anti-heterosexist arithmetic.

(Palmer 1986, p. 162)

Such associations between anti-racism, anti-heterosexism and the so-called 'loony left' were not confined to books with a relatively small circulation, but were also made in the popular press and the *TES* (see, for example, 10.1.86) and, of course, by Margaret Thatcher at the Conservative Party Conference in 1987:

Children who need to be able to count and multiply are learning anti-racist mathematics — whatever that may be. Children who need to be able to express themselves in clear English are being taught political slogans. Children who need to be taught to respect traditional moral values are being taught that they have an inalienable right to be gay.

The effect of such associations has been to make it easier for those teachers opposed to anti-racist education to dismiss it as being part of 'loony left' politics. For example, in one school where a number of teachers were extremely hostile to the development of anti-racist education, one of them said, to general nods of agreement, 'We don't have a problem here. There aren't many coloured (sic) children, and they're perfectly happy. Next you'll be asking us to do something about homosexuals', with the clear implication that that clinched the argument. At the time it was difficult to take the issue up adequately. On the one hand, if we said that we supported anti-heterosexist work in schools, this would simply confirm the opinions of these teachers. On the other, if we said nothing, our silence was a form of collusion. Again, we were put on the defensive, with a resulting rightwards pull of the ground of the argument.

The shift towards managerial relationships in schools

The failure of the teachers' industrial action in the mid-1980s ushered in a period of increasing shift away from collegial and towards managerial relationships in schools. Indeed, the industrial action was in part the battleground over which the issue of how schools should be managed was fought, and the imposition of the Pay and Conditions Act in 1987 can be seen as a decisive defeat for notions of collegial and democratic management of schools. This was particularly noticeable in the primary sector, even in schools where the head spent a great deal of time and effort in trying to establish and retain democratic forms of management. As the head of one school explained to me:

> The industrial action was a big deal for me. I mean, I supported it, thought the unions were right in their demands, but my responsibility was for the children and that meant that at times I did things I wasn't happy with. I think the effects are still with us. Teachers, union members, resented me and it's taking a long time for that to disappear.

The shift towards managerialism has been strengthened by the implementation of LMS, with heads and governors having new powers to hire and fire staff, decide on salaries, and so on. All these factors mean that the nature of change in schools needs to be rethought, since much previous work has been based on the notion that change cannot be imposed successfully from above.

The long-term effect of this shift on the development of anti-racist education is still difficult to judge. However it is likely that the increasingly

31

hierarchical nature of schools — already highly differentiated in terms of status of their participants — will be an obstacle to the development of anti-racist initiatives in education. I do not think it possible to make a clear assessment of this yet. However, there are indications from my work that the more authoritarian and hierarchical a school, the less progress is likely to be made in developing anti-racist approaches (see, in particular, chapter 5).

Official counter-discourses in national politics

The Swann Report

Ever since the mid 1960s black parents and pressure groups have complained of discrimination against, and underachievement by, their children. In 1977 a Parliamentary Select Committee reported on discontent over a number of issues, including education, felt by the African-Caribbean community in Britain. This led to the establishment of the Committee of Inquiry in the Education of Children from Ethnic Minority Groups in 1979, chaired, in the first instance, by Antony Rampton and, from 1981, by Lord Swann.

The terms of reference for the Committee were:

> Recognising the contribution of schools in preparing all pupils for life in a society which is both multi-racial and culturally diverse, the Committee is required to:
>
> > review in relation to schools the educational needs and attainments of children from ethnic minority groups taking account, as necessary, of factors outside the formal education system relevant to school performance, including influences in early childhood and prospects for school leavers;
> >
> > consider the potential of instituting arrangements for keeping under review the education performance of different ethnic minority groups, and what those arrangement might be;
> >
> > consider the most effective use of resources for these purposes;
> >
> > and to make recommendations.
>
> (Committee of Inquiry into the Education of Children from Ethnic Minority Groups 1985, page vii)

The Committee's Interim Report (the Rampton Report) concluded that, while racism was not the only factor causing underachievement of 'West Indian' children, there were also:

> various ways in which racism in the broadest sense in both schools and society can have a bearing on the achievement of West Indian children. The recommendations which we offer in respect of particular aspects

of education, notably on the curriculum, books and teaching materials and teacher education, are intended to overcome the effects of racism. In isolation, however, these cannot be enough. Teachers should be prepared to examine and reappraise their own attitudes and actions in an effort to ensure that their behaviour towards and expectations of ethnic minority pupils are not influenced by stereotyped and negative views. They should also be willing to challenge manifestations of racism wherever they occur by, for example, making clear that racist name-calling both in the school playground and classroom in (sic) unacceptable. In short we are asking teachers to play a leading role in seeking to bring about a change in attitudes on the part of society as a whole towards ethnic minority groups.

(Committee of Inquiry into the Education of Children from Ethnic Minority Groups 1981, p. 14)

Thus the discourse of anti-racism found its way, for the first time, into an official government publication and was used by some LEAs to legitimate the development and publication of policy on education for racial equality. Thus, although the Swann Report was heavily (and rightly) criticised for its individualisation of racism and relative lack of attention to it, it did provide a peg on which to hang anti-racist developmental work in schools. This peg has now been removed and, whilst anti-racist education continues to be necessary (since racism has not been eliminated from the education system) it is now undoubtedly more difficult (but not impossible) to find suitable replacements.

Thatcherism and the education market

The influence of both the neo-liberal and the traditionalist wings of the New Right on Thatcherite education policies is clearly demonstrated in a number of aspects of the ERA. Ball (1990b) quotes Baroness Cox as saying in interview, that:

... we tried to think how do you implement those in policy terms, taking those fundamental Conservative values. And those are the kind of values that are, I think, being developed in its policy proposals, and in Gerbil (Great Education Reform Bill). It would be surprising if there wasn't a congruence [with New Right thinking]. Those ideas are part of a changing climate of opinion and a changing political climate. Obviously many tributaries go into that river.

(p. 44)

Neo-liberalism has been most clearly expressed in terms of the creation of an 'education market' (Ball 1990a). This market has been institutionalised in a number of ways. Firstly, there is the establishment of parental 'choice' through open enrolment. However, it should be noted that such 'choice' will not be equally available to all, since the ability to 'choose' schools at a distance from home is confined to those who are able to provide time and transport to take their children to school. Secondly, competition between schools has been introduced through the same device. Thirdly, a number of new kinds of school have been introduced through arrangements for opting out and the establishment of City Technology Colleges (CTCs). Finally, new arrangements for funding will mean that the amount of money available to schools will be directly related to their success in attracting pupils.

Traditional conservatism, on the other hand, is best expressed through the National Curriculum, and, in particular, History, in which:

> ... At the very time when the Council of Europe (hardly a hot-bed of revolution) is calling for a move from history presented 'mainly from a national point of view', to one where the greater European and World context of developments is brought into the subject (Report of the Directorate of Education, Culture and Sport section for Council for Cultural Co-operation and Educational Research, October 1990), the Secretary of State for Education is asking that school history be re-written with a strong emphasis on British History and factual knowledge.
>
> (Bourdillon 1991, p. 17)

The ERA can, then, be seen as an attempt to 'go back to Victorian values' — which, despite their emotional appeal to certain politicians, are a mythology, an imaginary 'golden age' which it would be impossible to regain even had it ever existed. It can also be seen as an attempt to modernise and market schooling in ways which are anti-democratic, notwithstanding the appropriation of words like 'choice' and 'freedom' by the right. These tendencies are often contradictory and result in a tension which has yet to work its way through the education system, though cracks have already begun to appear.

References for Chapter 3

1. This has been done by a number of other authors, notably Cultural Studies, Birmingham (1991), Ball (1990a and 1990b), Jones (1989), Dale (1989).

2. And, it must be said, in Labour rhetoric too — see, for example, Labour's 1990 policy document, *Looking to the Future*, where it is stated that 'Our objectives in education and training are ambitious. We want to make the British people the best educated and trained in Europe' (p. 11).

3. At the time of writing the CRE are considering whether or not to appeal against this judgement.

4. I use the suffix 'men' deliberately here, although I recognise that there are (a small number) of businesswomen too. However, neo-liberals invariably talk about and interpellate 'men'.

5. However, discourses of derision and Conservative education policy have had their effect. According to a survey of teachers reported in the *TES* on 27 March 1992, 51% said they would vote Labour, 24% Liberal Democrat and only 20% Conservative.

6. For example, Anthony Flew, Anthony O'Hear (appointed to the Council for the Accreditation of Teacher Education in February 1991), Dennis O'Keeffe, John Marks, Ray Honeyford have all written in *TES* on a regular basis. It is perhaps worth noting that, in my search of the press, the earliest reference I found to the 'loony left' was in the *TES* on 10 January 1986 in an edition which contained several pages of attack by different authors on the left in the NUT, academia and politics.

7. The *TES* in this period is peppered with adverse articles about anti-racism. Representative examples can be found on 10.1.86, 17.1.86, 24.1.86, 12.9.86, 7.11.86.

8. The terminology adopted in Warwickshire is actually 'inter-cultural education'.

9. See Stacey (1991) for a fuller discussion of this point.

CHAPTER FOUR

POLITICAL DEBATE?

Labour movement pragmatism

The Labour Party

As we saw in the previous chapter, one result of the political hegemony of the right wing of the Conservative Party during the 1980s was a shift rightwards in political debate in England. This was achieved partly through the influence of the New Right and partly through choices made by, in particular, the Labour Party and the trade union movement to occupy much the same ground as the government (see Jones 1989).

Very little has been written about the Labour Party and New Realism in the 1980s. This omission is understandable in the light of the major impact which the New Right has had on education policy and the fact that 'New Realists' have themselves not produced a body of writing for analysis. However, I believe that this omission has led to a tendency to underestimate both the role that the Labour movement (that is, the Labour Party and the trade union movement) has had in allowing the debate to be very much located on ground laid out by the New Right and the effect of New Realism on the development and implementation of policies of local councils where the Labour Party has had control.

While the project of the Labour movement leadership is labelled 'New Realism', it has its origins much earlier and, in education, can be seen even before Callaghan's famous Ruskin speech in 1976 (Ball 1990b, pp. 30-34). However, determination to drive out the 'hard left' — represented in the popular press and by the Labour leadership as the Militant Tendency or the 'loony left' — and to become 'electable' was given a further edge by Labour's third defeat in a General Election in 1987. The fact that there appeared, in that and the previous election, to be a distinct 'London tendency' to vote against Labour lent further weight to the idea that left-wing politics — and specifically anti-racist and anti-heterosexist policies — lost elections. Since the Greater London Council under Ken Livingstone's leadership was renowned for its commitment to developing policies for equality —

37

especially in terms of race and sexuality — such policies were accepted by the Labour leadership as being vote-losers.[1] Thus the last years of the 1980s saw the virtual demise of 'Bennite' thinking within the Labour Party and the increasing hegemony within the party of the Kinnock leadership. In education, this showed itself as an increasing tendency to adopt the same ground as the Tory Government (Hillcole Group 1991, pp. 37-38).

Ken Jones (1989) argues that:

> The present shape of Labour's education policy cannot be understood without reference to the steady revision of platform and presentation that Labour's leadership believes is necessary to win an election after ten or a dozen years of Conservative rule: the celebrated new realism. The 'conditions of possibility' of new realism are the defeats suffered by militant trade unionism and by the left in the party, whose enthusiasms are blamed for the scale of the last two electoral disasters. It is far more however than a tactical realignment of platform: its rethinking has developed, unevenly and often in piecemeal ways, to extend to a range of strategic and philosophical issues which bear directly on present and future education policy. At its base it is possible to detect three related beliefs: one about the nature of contemporary capitalism; the second about the nature of a possible British socialism; the last about the means and agency of social change.

(p. 142)

Jones suggests that the Labour leadership accepts 'the predominant role of the market', believing that 'post- Fordist' society renders inappropriate older collectivised models for action and politics. This, he claims, leads them to develop a theory of British socialism which proposes that the task is to 'develop a programme of what Bryan Gould calls a 'Socialist modernisation" which would stress individual rights and give 'employees a 'stake in the productive process" (p.143). Jones identifies the third belief of the New Realists as being that:

> change [will be] carried out by governments and councils that do not reflect union struggles or turbulent movements for qualitative change, but rather implement a programme of moderate reform that is much more sensitive than the Labourism of the past to the views and pressures of non-union constituencies, and that wins electoral success by forsaking too close an involvement with producer groups.

(p. 144)

I would argue that this is an ideology of expediency based on 'commonsense' and pragmatic notions of what might make the Labour Party electable, rather than on thought out ideological positions developed by New Realist theorists and intellectuals. Nevertheless, I would agree with much of Jones' analysis of the different strands in New Realist thinking and with his assertion that, for education, they represent 'an updated but selective development of powerful elements in the Labour tradition' (p. 145).

The role of the Labour Party and trade union movement

The Tyndale affair in 1974 – 76, marked a qualitative defeat for progressive and radical ideas about education, which facilitated, though it did not cause, attempts to restructure education away from teacher control and towards central direction (Dale 1989). Dale points out two major outcomes of the public representation of the affair as follows:

> First, I think it made a major contribution to the articulation of 'parent power' to a conservative rather than a progressive or radical educational programme. ...

> Secondly, the scapegoating of the education system for the nation's economic failures need not necessarily have led to the teacher sector of the system taking all the blame.

> (pp. 145- 146)

The immediate effect of the Tyndale affair was in terms of attacks on performance of teachers and, in particular, on educational 'progressivism'.

Overall, the Tyndale affair gave a powerful justification to right-wing ideologues, such as Rhodes Boyson, in their attacks on teachers, (CCCS 1981). These attacks were not effectively opposed by either the NUT, which chose not to defend the Tyndale teachers, or the Labour Party, which has followed its own line of attacking teachers, starting with Callaghan's Ruskin Speech and pursued with vigour by successive Labour spokespeople on education. Moreover, the Labour Party leadership did not see education as an important political issue until late in 1989. At the Labour Party Conference in 1988 (the year of the ERA), the only debate on education lasted a mere twenty minutes and much of this time was taken up by a speech from Neil Fletcher (at that time Leader of ILEA), attacking teachers for falling standards in education. In the other main speech in this 'debate', Jack Straw (the front bench spokesperson on education) said that Labour supported the National Curriculum (and had thought of it first) and was not opposed to national tests (*TES* 7.10.88).

In the 1970s and 80s, Labour's concerns about education did not include any serious thinking about underlying principles. The comprehensive debate was never taken beyond a commitment to ending the 11 plus and introducing comprehensive secondary schools by Labour. Debate about education within the Labour Party following the Ruskin Speech was dominated by a preoccupation with structures and resources, and remained devoid of any discussion about what education should be like. Thus, although there was a commitment to equalising opportunity through the creation of comprehensive schools, this was seen in terms of widening a ladder to success, so that more children could succeed, but some would, inevitably continue to fail. Furthermore, the pragmatic tradition of the right-wing of the Labour Party, developed and re-labelled New Realism during the Thatcher years, lent itself to a form of politics in which seeking votes was more important than thinking about policies from theoretical or ideological perspectives. Thus, as was pointed out as early in the life of the Thatcher government as 1981, 'the more formed responses which have come from the Labour Party have been piecemeal and conservative' (CCCS 1981, p. 254). The tendency identified by CCCS has been intensified over the last decade, during which the search by the Labour leadership for popular policies has become ever more desperate. This is one reason why, when Joseph, and then Baker, became Secretaries of State with strong right-wing ideological notions about education, Labour had no thought-out alternative to offer.

Furthermore, Labour's lack of theoretical consideration of education as a political issue was echoed within the NUT and NASUWT. Even among the ranks of those union activists committed to some form of 'progressivism', the dominant concern was very much about pay and conditions rather than about education. Consequently the organisations that might have spearheaded the development of a real alternative to ERA were simply not in a position to do so.

Thus the 'New Realism' of the Labour Party and the TUC, including both the NUT and NASUWT, has meant that there has been little debate, on the national stage, about the purposes of education. Indeed, in 1990 Jack Straw held a joint press conference with John MacGregor, at that time Secretary of State for Education, which the *Guardian* reported in the following terms:

> Mr Straw could be seen wielding a red pen over his speech as he listened to Mr MacGregor telling the conference of the need to train pupils to become the good citizens of tomorrow. He needed to change what he had written because it was so closely in agreement with the minister.

(quoted in Hatcher 1990, p. 29)

The result of all this has been a pull to the right of debates on education at a national as well as a local level. While there has been protest from the NUT and the Labour Party about many of the measures of the ERA, this has been combined with accommodation to it.

The anti-racist movement and ERA

The accommodation to ERA prevalent within the labour movement has also been apparent amongst anti-racists. For example, Beverley Anderson, in her keynote address to the 1989 annual conference of the National Anti-racist Movement in Education (NAME), stressed what could be done within the confines of the ERA rather than possibilities for subverting its intentions (Anderson 1989), and Eggleston, speaking at NAME a year later, said, 'We must make the Act work for anti-racist education and achievement for all and use every means to adapt it, modify it, exploit it, and to make it happen' (Eggleston 1990, p.11). Furthermore, while there are problems with the Eurocentric nature of the National Curriculum, the real damage to educational equality will derive from differential resourcing of schools through LMS and opting out, which will exaggerate existing differences between 'haves' and 'have nots'.

Debate in schools

The introduction of National Curriculum has had contradictory effects on staff room discussions. In those schools where ideas about education were seldom or never discussed (but individual children were), teachers may have begun to share ideas about pedagogy and curriculum content for the first time. In others there has been a reduction in debate about educational issues which have been replaced by concern about the practicalities of, for example, Standard Assessment Tasks (SATS).

Another aspect of the impact of the growing influence of the New Right in education policy, is that teachers have felt themselves to have fewer and fewer options about curriculum and pedagogy. With the beginning of the implementation of the National Curriculum, this has become particularly marked but even before that there were changes in the degree of autonomy teachers had, or perceived themselves to have. In 1988, for example, the head of 'Badminton' School said that he did not feel able to make any far-reaching changes to the curriculum of his school until he had seen what the demands of the National Curriculum would be:

> It's no good making these changes now, if we'll only have to change again next year or the year after to accommodate the National Curriculum

(Diary July 1988).

While, on one level, this could be seen as a way of avoiding anti-racist change in the school — and there are schools which have tried to fit the National Curriculum into their existing practice rather than *vice versa* — he did also have a genuine concern about overloading his teachers and confusing his pupils by making frequent changes. This point will be further discussed below.

Another constraint has been the widespread demoralisation of teachers — demonstrated, in part, by the high level of resignations from teachers during 1989 and the large number of those remaining who were reported as saying that they would leave the profession if they could. The experience of the teachers' dispute was one demoralising event — particularly because it ended in defeat. However, another major factor has been the constant attacks by the media and politicians of both the Conservative and the Labour Party. These attacks have taken place on a number of levels — from the accusations of political bias and indoctrination discussed above, to the assumption that teachers are responsible for the supposed fall in reading standards. However, it would be wrong to believe that the picture of demoralisation is uniform across all schools. Some heads and teachers have managed to keep their enthusiasm going in spite of everything.

Accountability and public relations[2]

These attacks on teachers have a direct bearing on the importance which heads, in particular, attach to 'public relations'. In this sense, national politics and particularly 'discourses of derision' have influenced the ways in which schools represent themselves to their constituencies. These discourses have been both the result and the cause of widespread disaffection with schools and teachers and have had implications for both national policies and local actions. The success of the discourses in capturing the popular imagination has often worked through the publicising of particular local cases, which have then assumed national significance and had direct and indirect effects on education policy. They have also raised, in an acute form, the need to consider issues of accountability and its difference from exercises in public relations.

Accountability and Common-sense

In thinking about common-sense notions of accountability, several versions spring to mind. Sending an account involves a demand for payment and accountants 'do the accounts'. To account for one's actions necessitates offering some kind of explanation. The dictionary definition of 'accountable' is 'liable to account, responsible; explicable', while one of several definitions of 'account' is 'to give a reason or explanation'. However, one of the most important senses of 'giving an account' involves narrative — telling a story — and there is a sense in which all the other versions involve so doing. The narrative may be one of how money was spent and made (as in accountancy) or one of how certain events came about (as in explanation). What is rarely obvious in such definitions is any notion of power relations or of to whom accountability is owed and to whom holds oneself accountable.

It is these issues I wish to address, both questioning conservative (and Conservative) notions of accountability and raising the possibility of expanding the definition in such a way that, rather than a narrative being rendered after the event, it is developed in collaborative and co-operative ways during its making. However, it is not just that 'being accountable' or 'giving account' of oneself involves narrative. It is of key importance, particularly in the context of promoting equality, to consider to whom the narrative is told, as well as why and how it is told, for the answers to these questions can act as indices of relationships of power. If accountability is always 'upwards' in the hierarchy of institutions then, by definition, it cannot be a step towards democratising such organisations.

Neither is it possible to conceive of the promotion of equality within an accountancy model of accountability, for the market, by necessity, implies inequality (although a notion of equity, in the sense of getting a fair deal for your money, may exist). It is only when accountability is conceived of as part of a democratising process, with particular regard being paid to sharing the development and telling of stories with and to people in marginalised groups and in ways which allow for change, that it can be regarded as anti-oppressive. I would argue, further, that democratising institutions is not possible in the absence of such a process of accountability as narration with, as well as to, all the constituencies involved in the making and use of the institution.

Accountability in Education Policy

Conservative notions of accountability take two forms: market forces (and the accountability of the accountant) and hierarchical accountability to those in higher echelons of the institutions — hence the current stress on appraisal. ERA made schools accountable in the sense that, if they did not attract enough 'custom', they would lose pupils, and that publication of test results would reveal how well they were doing. However, we have seen that the marketplace, by definition cannot produce equality. Furthermore, under ERA, local control is exercised within a rigid framework imposed by the National Curriculum and the perils of funding. Furthermore under the 1986 Education Act 'local businesses' are to be strongly represented on the new governing bodies and the police consulted about the education of children (Jones 1989, Ball 1990a and 1990b). This, then, is the accountability of the market place and the accountant.

The other version of Conservative accountability can be seen at work in policies about appraisal, in which it is to be carried out exclusively by people in positions higher up in the hierarchies of educational institutions. Such accountability is to carried out after the event. Senior teachers will appraise junior teachers, heads will appraise senior teachers and will themselves be appraised by inspectors and so on. Eventually, payment will be based on the results of the appraisals (as well as on the judgement of the market). Even the retention of a teacher's job can now be based on such appraisal (*Times Educational Supplement* 6.3.92). This, then, is upwards accountability.

What current education policies do not contain is any notion of allowing students a say in their education or allowing parents the power to do more than manage a limited budget and vote for opting out of local authority control. Moreover, the parents to whom schools were to be held 'accountable' were those representing '*a particular version* of parenthood — the parent who owns his (sic) children, the parent who consumes education' (Johnson 1991a, p. 76, emphasis in original). [3] In this version of accountability, as Johnson (*ibid,* pp. 75-76) argues, teachers are to be held accountable only to those parents who agree with philosophies of competition and individualism. Those to whom these philosophies are anathema, who prefer democracy and co-operation, are constructed as 'other' and subversive.

The exclusion of certain groups of parents from Conservative notions of accountability can be seen particularly clearly in the naming (in Section 28 of the Local Government Act 1988) of lesbian and gay parents and their children as 'pretended families'. These parents' preference for their children and their children's peers to receive an education providing positive images of lesbians and gays are ruled out of court without further consideration. Boundaries are thus drawn between those parents to whom educational institutions are legitimately held accountable and those to whom they are not.

Another group of parents clearly excluded from the availability of 'choice' are those Muslim parents who wish to see the establishment of separate state-funded schools for their children. The point here is not whether separate schools are desirable, but that in refusing to allow their establishment, the government has made a clear statement that Muslim parents are not to have the same degree of 'market choice' as those groups for whom voluntary aided schools already exist. For these parents, then, this version of accountability is a dead letter.

The contradictory nature of Conservative versions of accountability can be seen clearly in the case of the opted-out school in Stratford East, where some of the parent governors wished to dismiss the head for allegedly racist actions. The point here is not the truth or otherwise of the allegations, important though this is, but the eventual decision by the government that the views of the parents were to be dismissed and the head of the school kept in post (*Guardian* 6.3.92 and 7.3.92). In this case accountability to that particular group of parents was rejected in favour of upwards accountability. The resignation of some of the governors involved in this case does not change the basic point being made.

Neither are children or older students seen as 'consumers' to whom the 'producers' of education should be accountable. In terms of the Education Reform Act, pupils and students are seen as 'commodities' and, in training for school governors, have indeed been described as such.[4]

Furthermore, schools and teachers are to be held accountable to government for the transmission of those preselected knowledges contained in the National Curriculum. This is to take precedence over any wish on the part of parents for an alternative curriculum, unless, of course, they happen to have sent their children to public schools, which are exempt from such demands. There is, furthermore, considerable pressure on teachers and teacher educators to adopt models of pedagogy which assume that students are empty vessels to be filled up and that there is absolutely no necessity for negotiation between teachers and students.

The main features of Conservative accountability are, then, contained in notions of appraisal and marketability. Ball (1990b) points out that 'marketisation' of schools is constructed through particular discourses about school 'effectiveness':

> Effectiveness researchers both construct a concept of the ineffective or sick school and draw upon the use of confessional techniques (an admission of transgressions and a ritual of atonement) as a mechanism for the return to health or to a state of grace. The school is to take responsibility for its ailments and its own cure. (p. 90)

He argues further that 'the thrust of effectiveness is the limitation of the range of possibilities for normal education' (p.90). I would wish to add to this that accountability through appraisal is also carried out through discourses of school effectiveness. This is important when thinking about the development of anti-oppressive education — will/can it be within the range of discursive possibilities available in the context of marketisation and appraisal on the basis of particular notions of 'effectiveness' based on the publication of test results? The apparent objectivity of tests is important here as a legitimising force establishing marketisation as a (perhaps the) most favoured method of assessing schools.

Accountability or Public Relations?

The rhetoric of accountability has become part of the language of educational discourse. I would argue that, as in the marketing of commercial products, the concept of accountability usually adhered to is one which is more akin to public relations than to a democratisation of the way schools are actually managed. Glossy school prospectuses have become the order of the day, and heads are ever more anxious to gain favourable publicity for their schools in the local press and radio. While this is an understandable reaction to changes in education policy, such actions, in the absence of democratising versions of accountability, are unlikely to lead to any greater satisfaction with their schools on the part of students or parents.

Fletcher et al (1985 pp. 123-4) point out that a failure in public relations has been a feature of a number of *causes célèbre* in education and that they frequently mark the 'boundaries to development' of a particular educational principle, though it is usually a particular incident apparently unconnected with the deeper principle which triggers such public controversy. For example, at Risinghill in 1961, a survey on racism led to a major scandal whose underlying cause turned out to be sex education, while at Countesthorpe in 1973, lessons about swearing were the basis for an attack on independent learning.

Thus public relations is a legitimate part of the role of heads — and good public relations are, perhaps, even more important when a school embarks on a process of innovation. However, as Ball (1987, pp 250-253) points out, such public controversies come to a head when the various constituencies of a school are divided amongst themselves: for example, the Tyndale affair was sparked off by a discontented teacher; at Risinghill and Countesthorpe the LEA inspectorate were in disagreement with the school; the major attacks on Culloden School in 1991 were facilitated by the dissatisfaction of some parents with their children's progress at school.[5] Such conflicts are used by local and national media to orchestrate public 'trials'. All these cases illustrate ways in which conflict at the micro-political level can become implicated in developments at the macro-political level. More importantly, they demonstrate the need for the kind of accountability which involves negotiation and dialogue, and represents a move towards the democratisation of education. Such a move would obviously not eliminate conflict, but it might well reduce its damaging effects.

Successful public relations are not a substitute for negotiation between the teachers and the other constituencies of the school. Johnson (1991b) argues that public professionals, including teachers, can use their power oppressively, often defining their own failures as the failures of their clients (or, in the case of teachers, their students) and that this:

> ... [supplies] Thatcherism with political resources. There are accumulated popular injuries here. There is enough truth in New Right charges against public professionals to make them stick, even though professionals rarely control the financial and other parameters. Antagonisms between clients and state professionals can be given as much significance as conflicts between working people and their employers, or between men, women and children in domestic relations. *Causes célèbre* like the Cleveland child abuse cases[6] and more routine denigration (sic) of teachers or social workers are cases in point.
>
> (p. 109)

It is certainly true that the government has been able to use genuine discontent amongst parents and students about education, which has been exacerbated by the widespread failure of teachers to hold themselves accountable to anyone but themselves. This failure has been particularly apparent in relation to the education of black children (Coard 1971, Stone 1981) but extends also to other children and parents, and teachers themselves feel it when they themselves are also parents. Thus, when Kenneth Baker introduced the Education Reform Bill following the re-election of the Conservative government in 1987, he was able to appeal to a wellspring of support for 'accountability' and local control.

In terms of the development of anti-racist education, the danger is that the possibility of bad publicity, like that given to Brent LEA and to the work of our project when it hit national and local headlines in August 1987, will deter heads from undertaking or allowing such initiatives to take place in their schools.

Publicity and my project

In the case of the project on which I was engaged, the media attacks were led by the *Daily Mail* (28.8.87), which quoted Dame Jill Knight as saying that 'Wherever small children are being indoctrinated in this way there is a strong and totally understandable adverse reaction'. The *Mail* article was followed by similar coverage in other national dailies and the local press. The project was reported as introducing the counting of yams and pomegranates instead of apples and pears (which hardly seems offensive, though it was an inaccurate account of what we were trying to do). As a result of these press reports, the British National Party began a campaign in the locality reported under the headline 'Anger over 'indoctrination' of alien cultures..' and handed out leaflets in the area (but outside the wrong schools!) claiming that the project was:

> to ensure that our kids should be BRAINWASHED with Communist 'one-world' PROPAGANDA. ... It would be interesting to know the 'ethnic' background of these people, chances are they are not English!
>
> (BNP leaflet, September 1987)

It is certainly the case that some of the heads with whom we discussed the possibility of our working in their schools demurred on the grounds of the potential bad publicity for the school. This could have been indication of an unwillingness to engage in anti-racist change and/or a genuine fear about what such publicity might lead to. It was, however, not a universal reaction and the head and teaching staff of 'Badminton' School (where we were working at the time) reacted to adverse comment from the media by becoming even more determined to pursue the work of the project. As I wrote in my research diary:

> [Following the publicity in the national and local press] we went into school feeling extremely nervous. We spent some time discussing it with [the head] who expressed his anger at what had happened and his determination not to let it deter him. Later in the day, we had discussions with the rest of the staff, who all agreed that they wished to carry on with the Project and would not allow themselves to be put off. Susan said that she was 'damned if she would let them get away with it'. There has been no reaction from any of the parents yet, though [the head] did receive a call from the Chair of Governors asking him what it was all about.

Determination to 'carry on regardless' is not, however, an adequate solution. We need to find ways of demystifying education and for teachers, students and parents to engage in negotiations about the purposes, nature and content of education. The need for such negotiations has been mentioned above and it was demonstrated in the Burnage Report (Macdonald et al 1989). Negotiations of this kind are a clear part of any effective education for equality.

The point about adverse publicity is not simply that it has direct effects on possibilities for anti-racist development. This coverage was part of the way in which anti-anti-racism was constructed and popularised and had more indirect and subtle effects than the immediate ones. The construction of discourses about racism and anti-racism affected and limited the possibilities open to teachers. National policies and major public discourses were, in very important senses, the material with which we and the teachers with whom we collaborated could work. The ways in which we worked with them was not predetermined but we could not step outside the political context to avoid engaging with national policies and public discourses, though our work could take the form of deconstruction and resistance. It is also important to note that local initiatives and demands can and do lead to changes in national political debates and policies. For example, demands for separate schools by groups of black parents (particularly Muslims) and their attempts, formulated locally, to use the provisions of the ERA to obtain grant maintained status, have clearly put this issue on the agenda of national debate about education policy. Similarly, what began as local conflict in the Tyndale affair has, as Dale (1989, chapter 8) points out, had a lasting significance in the education politics of England.

The version of accountability enshrined in the ERA contains particular dangers for the development of education for equality. Reliance on marketability mean that initiatives designed to combat inequality are deprioritised by schools concerned about adverse publicity. The appeal of public relations must be to the maximum number of people and where the dominant ideologies and discourses are those of racism, sexism and heterosexism, such an appeal is unlikely to come from opposition to these ideologies. Nevertheless, it is important to note that counter-discourses are available and these can be seen in the references made by most National Curriculum Council documents to equal opportunities (even though it is used in a weak sense here). It is through these contradictions and through moving towards a democratic version of accountability that we will be able to develop anti-oppressive education.

Conclusion — ERA and the future

The success of the New Right

It is important to draw some lessons from the success of the New Right. This and the previous chapter have shown that the introduction of ERA was, to a great extent, an institutionalisation of an already existing climate, built up through attacks on state education and on teachers, which predates the election of the Thatcher government in 1979. It is important to note that, while the Pay and Conditions Act 1987 was coercive of teachers, much of the success of the New Right has been achieved through persuasion. People (many people) believe that standards have fallen, that anti-racism is undemocratic, that homosexuality is a perversion, and so on. Popular consent to these propositions has been gained through a populism based on real discontents — comprehensive schooling did not achieve equality — and a failure to offer alternative discourses by those forces potentially in a position to do so — the Labour Party and the NUT.

I have argued in this chapter that national politics have a direct bearing on the micro-politics of schools and, hence, on the ways in which school change. It is clearly the case that possibilities for the development of anti-racist education have been severely damaged by the influence of the New Right leading up to and including the imposition of ERA in 1988. Teachers, who were already demoralised by the stresses and failure of their industrial action, have been subjected to an ever-increasing stream of demands on them to change their schools. Moreover, the changes they have had to make have been ever more constraining in their effect on the options open to teachers wishing to introduce or develop anti-racist and anti-sexist education in their schools.

Does this mean that there is no future for anti-racist education in this country? I believe there is — for a number of reasons. Firstly, the National Curriculum and New Right thinking on education are not without their own contradictions, which can be exploited to develop alternatives. The New Right is, itself, divided on the issue of whether there should be a National Curriculum. Such centralising state control is contrary to their philosophy of the free market. Moreover, as Johnson (1991a, p.85) argues, the long-term effect of New Right ideologies is divisive and likely to heighten antagonisms which will, themselves, produce political dissent and resistance. This is already clearly apparent in relation to the National Health Service and has begun to develop in relation to education — although the fourth Conservative general election victory in April 1992 is an indication that dissent was not yet extensive enough to change people's votes in sufficient numbers (or in the key marginals) for a Labour victory or a hung parliament..

Secondly, the National Curriculum itself is not homogeneous. Clarke's adjustment of the geography curriculum, for example, is at odds with the National Curriculum Council's proposals for 'citizenship' and attention to social and environmental issues (NCC 1990). The Cox Report (NCC 1989) acknowledges bilingualism as something positive, while stressing the virtues of Standard English. Much depends on the development of alternative pedagogies (discussed in chapters 6 and 7) and on the micro-politics of individual schools (discussed in the next chapter).

References for Chapter 4

1. For example, early in 1987 Patricia Hewitt, then Neil Kinnock's press secretary, wrote to a right-wing Labour MP expressing concern that the 'gay and lesbian issue' was losing votes, especially amongst pensioners (*Guardian*, 7 March, 1987). Hewitt's previous record as General Secretary of the National Council for Civil Liberties (NCCL, now called 'Liberty') made this letter a matter of particular shock and concern, given NCCL's record of fighting for lesbian and gay rights.

2. For a more detailed discussion of issues of accountability in education (see Epstein 1992 and forthcoming).

3. Johnson's discussion of Conservative 'accountability' is particularly useful in analysing its nature in the ERA.

4. I am indebted to Barry Troyna for telling me about this description, given in a governors' training session in which he was taking part as a governor.

5. Culloden was the subject of a major television series, which followed events at the school over the year. It became the subject of attack when a journalist from the *Mail on Sunday* started phoning parents during half-term (18-22 February, 1991) and found 40 prepared to have their children's reading ability 'tested' by Martin Turner, the educational psychologist at the centre of attacks on the use of 'real books' in teaching reading.

6. It is, however, important to note that, though this is rarely reported, many of the 'Cleveland children' remained in care or subject to supervision orders following the Butler-Sloss enquiry and there are a number of prosecutions of fathers and other men still in progress.

CHAPTER FIVE

MICRO-POLITICS, COLLABORATIVE TEACHING AND SCHOOL CHANGE

This chapter develops a framework for examining school change and follows on with three case studies of schools in which I have worked, either as head of Infants or as a teacher adviser.

Perspectives on school change

'School improvement' and change

Michael Fullan (1985) summarises his findings about change in schools in the following list:

(1) that change takes place over time

(2) that the initial stages of any significant change always involve anxiety and uncertainty

(3) that on-going technical and psychological support and assistance is crucial if the anxiety is to be coped with

(4) that change involves learning new skills through practice and feedback — it is incremental and developmental

(5) that the most fundamental breakthrough occurs when people can cognitively understand the underlying conception and rationale with respect to 'why this new way works better'

(6) that organizational conditions within the school (peer norms, administrative leadership) and in relation to the school (e.g. external administrative support and technical help) make it more or less likely that the process will succeed

51

(7) successful change involves pressure, but it is pressure through interaction with peers and other technical and administrative leaders.

(p.396)

These perspectives, which derive primarily from the study of in-service work designed to improve schools' 'effectiveness',[1] offer some suggestions for the creation of change in schools. Many of Fullan's conditions for change appear to be 'common-sense'. However, his work and that of his colleagues in the International School Improvement Project does not provide a framework for examining the actual processes of change and of the ways in which change can be resisted as well as initiated.

Furthermore, I would suggest that there are specific issues related to change concerning equality which are not present, or at least not present in the same form, in issues concerning curriculum change and I would question whether it is possible to use Fullan's approach as the main way of creating or analysing anti-racist or anti-sexist developments. These issues relate in part to the hegemonic culture of racism and sexism in our society and to the way in which anti-racism has been constructed as being marginal by the Right and the popular media. What anti-racist change does share with curriculum change is that making a start is likely, at least in the first instance, to make severe demands on the professional and personal skills of the teacher (MacDonald 1973, Stenhouse 1980).

There seems to be an assumption in the writings of those involved in the 'school improvement' movement that change is, in itself, a 'good thing'. However, from the point of view of those wishing to increase equality in education, this is not necessarily the case. Some curriculum changes can be racist and sexist in effect, as is likely in the case of the introduction of the National Curriculum (see, for example, Troyna and Carrington 1990, especially chapter 6). Furthermore, changes intended to increase equality do not always work and, in some cases, the processes of change can be such that they are, in effect, counter-productive, as the report of the Burnage Inquiry suggested in relation to the 'top-down' imposition of anti-racist policies (Macdonald 1989). This chapter argues therefore, that the *process* of change is as important as any policy measures adopted and that developing anti-racist policies should be seen as a tool for facilitating change rather than viewing the policies as an end in themselves.

Micro-politics and school change

Stephen Ball's *The Micro-Politics of the School* (1987) broke new ground in developing ideas about how schools function. In acknowledging the influence of this book on my thinking, I would like to note that the differences in size and organisation between secondary and primary schools make a difference to the micro-politics of these institutions. Ball stresses the importance of examining the day-to day running of schools, looking at power relationships and conflicts within them and their particular histories, and he questions the value of:

the continually regurgitated motifs of macro versus micro, structure versus action, free will versus determinism, teachers versus the mode of production. In important ways this has led to both an under-emphasis on and a misrepresentation of other major arenas of analysis in sociological study — the work group and the organization — what might be called the meso-level.

(p. 3)

He raises issues about the control of schools which, he claims, are the subject of constant negotiation and renegotiation with shifting boundaries within schools and differing boundaries in different schools. In doing so he does not reject completely categories of analysis used by others, but uses them where appropriate for the particular situations he is discussing. He comments too on the diversity of goals amongst teachers and between schools and the impact of external, and often contradictory, demands and pressures from outside schools. He also points out that it is:

not only ... necessary to pay particular attention to the control and structure of organizational matters in school but also it is important to take account of the peculiar *content* of policy-making and decision-making in school. For a great deal of that content is *ideological.* ...

Clearly, not all decisions faced by head teachers or schools are ideological, but virtually all matters which relate to the organization and teaching of pupils, the structure of the curriculum, the relationships between teachers and pupils and the pattern of decision-making in the institution have strong ideological underpinnings.

(pp. 13-15, original emphases)

Ball offers a number of case studies through which he examines the politics of change in secondary schools and, in particular, the role of the head, the politics of age and gender, political leadership within schools and the impact on them of the 'outside world'. In doing so, he outlines a number of different styles of headship, an outline I have found particularly useful in looking at the management of anti-racist change in predominantly white primary schools. I develop Ball's framework here, looking at the specificity of change in relation to issues of race and at the effect of a school's history and existing customs and tradition on its micro-politics and, hence, the way change is experienced by its staff and students.

Lyseight-Jones (1989) suggests that there are internal and external pressures for change and that defining issues of race, racism and anti-racism is an important part of managing anti- racist school change since, as she says,

53

'incorrect or inadequate definition of the issue will lead to inappropriate outcomes' (p. 39).

She identifies, as the actors in the change process, the 'initiator', 'allies', 'blockers', 'opinion leaders', 'don't knows', 'laggards' and 'bandwagoners' (p.41). She further draws attention to the need to deal with different forms of opposition in different ways; for outside support, including high level legitimisation of developments; to the importance of the role of the head; and to good dissemination of information. Lyseight- Jones' more pragmatic approach, taken in conjunction with Ball's more theoretically rewarding discussion of a conflict perspective in the micro-politics of school change (Ball 1987, pp. 28-46), provides a fruitful framework for thinking about anti-racist change processes.

A framework for analysis

Whilst Ball's focus in *The micro-politics of the school* (1987) is a general analysis of school change, I have concentrated on an analysis of anti-racist change through micro-politics and collaborative teaching. Another difference between my research and that of Ball, is that whereas he was looking at given situations and examining how change occurred within them, my aim was the *creation* of change in a particular direction — that of anti-racist and anti-sexist education. The framework I have developed involves looking at the initial stages of development, including the use of INSET (In-Service Education of Teachers); the role of the head in the creation of change; the function of developing school policies; the relationship of key opinion leaders within the schools with each other and with myself and the processes involved in identifying these people; the identification of 'blockers' and 'allies'; and the need for some kind of yardstick against which to measure change.

Micro-politics and the Education Reform Act

Do micro-politics still matter?

It may seem that the ERA has had such an enormous effect on schools that micro-politics have become irrelevant. This, however, is far from being the case. The innovations called for by the Act can only be carried out by teachers working in schools with specific histories, power relationships and institutional arrangements. Consequently, the ways in which the provisions of the ERA will be implemented will depend on the micro-politics surrounding their introduction in particular schools.

Ball and Bowe (1991) point out that:

> ... implementation [of policy] is highly problematic, involving active processes of accommodation and mediation. And policy texts are often less that straightforward since they allow, often unintentionally, for variations and play. ...

> The responses of the schools to ... changes are dependent upon their varying interpretations of the ERA and their anticipation as to the effects of that policy upon them.
>
> (p. 23)

Ball and Bowe examine the implementation of the ERA and, in particular, the marketisation of schooling, in four secondary schools in two LEAs, showing just how much the schools differed as a result of their micro-politics. My field work took place before and during the introduction of the ERA. Thus, although the micro-politics of the schools in my study were partly shaped by the advent of ERA, its full impact was as yet unknown. Nevertheless the close examination of micro-political processes in these schools remains relevant, for although the macro-political conditions may have changed, these processes, involving relations of power, conflict and co-operation have continued.

Innovation Overload[2]

> Everybody seemed really worn down and exhausted at school today. [The head] has asked for a meeting to discuss how the school can ensure that the implementation of the National Curriculum doesn't damage anti-sexist and anti-racist strategies in the classroom, but it seems like a majority of the staff don't want yet another meeting. They have been meeting in year groups to look at their planning for next year in the light of the reports from the English, Maths and Science working parties.
>
> (Diary June 1989)

One of the factors which has very much affected the micro-politics of schools both before and since the ERA has been the number of new initiatives which teachers have been expected to undertake. Even before the advent of the National Curriculum these pressures were considerable. While a number of these demands related to secondary schooling (for example, GCSE and TVEI), primary schools also felt the effects of an increasing workload as they introduced new schemes of work, statementing of pupils with Special Educational Needs and the integration of such pupils into mainstream schooling, records of achievement, curriculum statements and so on. Since the introduction of the ERA the requirement to change has intensified enormously, as new National Curriculum Council reports, Orders in Council about different subjects and other documents requiring attention have arrived in schools at an overwhelming rate. This has had a marked effect on the working conditions of teachers, who have found that they need to spend more and more time on familiarising themselves with new requirements and that while their working hours may well have increased, an ever smaller proportion is spent actually teaching children.

In this context, many teachers felt that the introduction of anti-racist education was simply another innovation to cope with and, since it is not compulsory in the way that many of the other innovations are, have simply chosen not to take on yet another task. Even teachers and heads who previously saw themselves as committed to developing education for equality in their schools have often deprioritised these issues in favour of trying to implement the National Curriculum, manage their own budgets and deal with the implications of hiring and firing staff.

However, this is not universally the case. In some schools, teachers have attempted to make anti-racist and anti-sexist education an intrinsic part of their implementation of the National Curriculum, and this was the purpose of the head of Dover School in calling the meeting mentioned at the beginning of this section. Unfortunately, there are considerable problems with this approach because of the eurocentric and nationalistic nature of much of the National Curriculum. As Tim Brighouse said, we should not 'confuse providing the same thing to everyone with equal opportunity' (quoted in Jones 1990a). The Cox Report (NCC 1989), with its section on 'Equal opportunities' raised hopes that issues of race, gender and class might be dealt with. However, the section ends with the weakest possible statement on equality:

> The causes of such differences are not well understood. But curricular and assessment arrangements should aim to raise expectations and help to narrow the gap wherever possible.

> (para. 11.10)

Moreover in terms of issues of equality, this report is the strongest, of all the Reports of the Subject Working Groups. The nationalistic and restrictive nature of the National Curriculum has become more apparent with each successive report and the Government's reaction to it. Kenneth Clarke, for example, insisted that in the report on geography all political aspects be removed (*TES* 18.1.91).

Micro-politics and primary schools

The case studies contained in the rest of this chapter suggest that, while the role of the head is important in the micro-politics of anti-racist change in primary school, it is not the only factor involved. Equally important are the existing traditions and culture of the school, the role of initiators of change and group alliances which exist and develop during the process of change. Further, I would suggest that while micro-politics sometimes operate unconsciously — perhaps particularly in the primary sector where the myth of 'cosiness' is strong — change is best managed when conscious strategies are undertaken involving careful definition of the issues, taking opportunities which present themselves and planning ahead to build up alliances, deflect or pre-empt opposition and use whatever external pressures and supports are possible. It is also important to take into account the fact that the collegial pressures of primary schools may be such as to render staff meetings a poor forum for making grand policy statements and winning policies through debate. A less risky strategy, probably more effective in the long run than merely winning debates, is slow and patient work, preferably with the opportunity created for staff development through collaborative work.[3]

The case studies of all three schools discussed in the following pages appear to show quite clearly that primary schools do have a micro-politics, involving conflict and integration, alliances and interest groups, political activity and ideological disputation (Ball 1987, p. 8). It is, of course, likely that conflict will bear the weight of political stances and conflicts developed outside the school, resulting in processes of change and resistance to change being complex and multi-faceted. My case studies suggest that school change is a complicated process, requiring not only the active agency of some (influential) members of staff but also the management of both active and passive opposition.

Even writers publishing in the '90s (e.g. Grugeon and Woods 1990) seem to ignore completely the dimension of micro-politics in their discussions of anti-racist development in primary schools. By doing so, they over-simplify the processes and issues involved, reducing them to pedagogy and curriculum content. While both of these aspects are critically important, neglect of the micro-politics involved in getting appropriate pedagogies and curriculum content will leave those just beginning the process of change in the position of, perhaps, knowing what they want to achieve but with no way of getting there than by trial and error. It is essential to view every school as a site of struggle, where the negotiations taking place can either strengthen or weaken possibilities for developing education for equality.

Case Studies

1. Bankhead School — Working as an 'Insider'

'Bankhead' School is a large junior and infants school serving a large, newish Council estate in a shire county. This estate had very poor facilities. A relatively high proportion of fathers were unemployed. The school had few black children, but there was one black member of the Infant staff (Christine), and the head of Juniors (Louise) had black grandchildren and consequently a personal stake in the promotion of racial equality.

Initial stages

As head of Infants I was part of the senior management team of the school. The head who appointed me left at the end of my first term at the school. There followed six months with an acting head, after which the new head (Jack) took up his post. So the deputy (Thomas), Louise and I had to take considerable responsibility for the management of the school and we were able to influence developments when Jack became head, in a way which might not have been possible with an established head. Despite 'discourses of derision' and innovation overload, there was still a feeling of commitment among most of the teachers and a willingness to try new ideas in order to improve pedagogy and 'standards' in their classrooms. When I accepted the post of head of Infants, the school had, as yet, made no attempt to respond to the Swann Report (1985) by developing multicultural or anti-racist education.

The first phase in change consisted mainly of the gathering of allies, of informal discussions between certain members of the teaching staff, of getting to know the school and of establishing my own credibility as a teacher. I was aware, at this time, of several aspects of the organisation of the school which could be described as institutionally racist. For example, the few children for whom English was a second language were withdrawn from their classrooms in order to receive language support.[4] This contrasted strikingly with the policy of the school concerning children with Special Educational Needs, which was to provide mainstream support in the classroom and not withdraw children except for individual assessment by the Educational Psychologist or Special Needs Co-ordinator.

The anglocentric nature of the curriculum was another important aspect of institutional racism operating in the school. All the teachers were committed to 'child-centred' education, but all too often, 'starting with the child' meant failure to take the children beyond their own experience, to consider the experience of others or issues of power relating to race or gender. They also fail to recognise that 'child-centred' education which did not take account of the experience of black and other ethnic minority children was not 'child-centred' for those children. Their lives included a variety of experience — from speaking more than one language to coping with racial harassment — which an education based on assumptions about the experience of white working class children could not possibly include.

Along with the absence of any reference to black experience in the taught curriculum, was implicit denial of the existence of black people in the posters and other resources used in the school, For example, dolls in the infant classrooms were all white; music in assemblies was generally European and classical. The issue of having black dolls was one of the first which I took up. I had some money to spend on re-equipping the play houses in the Infant classrooms and wanted to buy black dolls for each classroom. My suggestion met with opposition, though it was not strongly expressed directly to me nor raised in staff meetings as a problem, and I proceeded to order the dolls. The incident did not seem to me to be of great significance, but, two years later, it stood out in the memories of the teachers as enormously important.

In retrospect, I can see that the decision was symbolic, visible and lasting — one which made a statement to parents as well as to teachers and children. Secondly, it made it clear to other members of staff that I regarded issues of race as high priority, so had the effect of heightening their own consciousness, even if, at first, this took the form of being careful about what they said in my presence. It is important to note that, had I not been in a position of senior management, the opposition to the purchase would almost certainly have been voiced more strongly, the black dolls not bought — and the issue being forgotten or buried. Had a probationary teacher for example, made the suggestion and it was rejected out of hand, she would be unlikely to raise issues of race again in the near future. It is also important to realise that I did not, at the time, invest my decision with such crucial importance. It seemed to me to be a relatively small step, one which could be taken very easily.

Micro-politics, then, does not always operate at a conscious level. It is not the case that every action and step on the way to creating change must be, or even can be, consciously and carefully planned. Sometimes the courses of action which turn out to be effective, such as the purchase of black dolls, are generated by a combination of intuition about what is important and good luck. Timing is also important and this too is frequently a case of chance and good fortune (or mischance and ill fortune).[5]

Allies

As I became integrated into the school, most of the influence I had was due to taking the opportunities which arose rather than to a premeditated strategy. I did not, at that point, have a worked-out strategy of finding allies, identifying blockers, and so on but, as a new member of staff looked for like-minded people to relate to and was fortunate that one of my strongest supporters was Louise. Thomas was active in the NUT and he too was sympathetic to ideas of anti-racist education, in line with union policy. The fact that all three of the existing senior management had some commitment to anti-racist education meant that it was easy to ensure that issues of race and racism remained on the agenda.

With the appointment of Jack as the new head came the second phase in the development of anti-racist education at the school. I raised the issue in a senior management meeting, and it was agreed that a working party be set up to produce a discussion document on anti-racist education.

The discussion was then delayed, because I had to go into hospital, but I was assured that it would continue when I returned. In fact this hiatus possibly worked to the advantage of the development of anti-racist education in Bankhead School, since the first Multicultural Adviser for the county took up his appointment while I was still on sick leave. I was able to make an early appointment to meet him to discuss a number of issues, including the possibility of his playing a role as an external agent at the school when it became appropriate. It turned out that his intervention was a crucial factor in the later adoption by the school of anti-racist guidelines. Again the importance of luck, timing and chance in the operation of micro-politics can be seen. There was no way that I could have deliberately organised my hospitalisation in such a way as to give me time for informal contact with the new Multicultural Adviser.

Lyseight-Jones (1989, p. 49) draws attention to the need for 'high level legitimization' in developing anti-racist education, and the Multicultural Adviser certainly provided this. My own experience of interviewing teachers (Epstein 1991) confirmed that this was the case, both in terms of legitimation and in combating feelings of isolation. My contact with the Multicultural Adviser provided both of these and I was further supported at a personal level through my involvement in the National Anti-Racist Movement in Education.

Strategies for change

When I returned from sick leave, members of the senior management team knew that the development of an anti- racist/multicultural policy would be high on the agenda for staff meetings. I had also spent a great deal of time in discussion with other members of staff over the period I was at the school, in particular with two of the younger teachers (Jane and Lorna) with whom I used to drive to school each day. These informal discussions (another example of chance) were extremely important. They ranged over a number of issues in education and often centred on racism, both overt and covert.

Such 'backstage' discussions are a key element of micro-politics. Through them people build up shared commitments and a constituency begins to be built for pushing forward particular ideas and interpretations. Jane and Lorna became firm allies in the attempt to develop anti-racist education at the school. Christine, who had hitherto taken a very low profile on issues of race, now began to discuss them more readily. This change in her willingness to discuss racism was partly an indirect result of the discussions in the car, since these conversations led to her being invited to comment on her experience of racism by Jane and Lorna in a way that they had not previously done. Christine possibly also gained confidence from her own promotion. Two teachers (Sharon and Rose) were actively hostile and the rest were unsure, but felt challenged by the issues being raised.

On my return to school I took on the role of 'floating' teacher. This was a role I had requested: it would give me the opportunity to work collaboratively with every teacher in the school; to find out what was happening in each unit; and to establish my reputation as a 'good teacher' and supportive colleague in ways that are impossible when tied to one class. This credibility as a teacher is very important in initiating change. Without it, other teachers can easily reject the new ideas out of hand. I was also able to take every opportunity to introduce anti-racist and multicultural approaches in all the classrooms. For example, some teachers started to use a variety of different languages for calling the register and found that the children responded very well to this, and that two bilingual children were teased far less about their language. The school's ethos was, generally, beginning to change.

At the same time as I began teaching collaboratively, as the 'floating' teacher in all the units in the school, we started a pre-school group, which opened once a week for children under five and their carers. I ran this group with a newly appointed part-time teacher and a nursery nurse. This teacher was an experienced teacher of English as a Second Language, and had knowledge of, and commitment to, anti-racist education. Through the group we were able to involve a number of mothers in the life of the school, including three black women. One of them expressed to us her unhappiness at her children's rejection of Gujerati when they started school. Another spoke of her child's attendance at Arabic classes. Both talked of their experience of racism.

Because of my growing relationship with these women, I was able to express my ideas to staff through examples drawn from the experiences of children whom they knew, taught and were concerned about, and this had a noticeable effect on some teachers' receptiveness to these ideas. The pre-school group was also a forum for discussion and developing relationships with the white parents and child-minders who came to it and, while listening to and discussing their problems as a group, the white mothers were also able to listen to the black women. This was important in that it provided a basis of parental support for the development of anti-racist policies[6] — although, of course, it would be unrealistic to say that everyone involved became a committed anti-racist.

Ball (1987) comments that staff meetings provide the main arena for debate in schools (p.39) and this may apply in large secondary schools where the possibilities for developmental work through personal contact and collaborative teaching are, perhaps, limited. However, I would suggest that it is less likely in the primary school, where staff meetings do not take on the aspect of the large public meeting because of the smaller size of the schools. My strategy was more in the style which Ball labels 'interpersonal',[7] and relied on the slow work of persuasion, not simply through discussion but, most importantly, through shared practice and reflection on it. By the time the issues came to a staff meeting enough progress had been made through persuasion and strong enough alliances built with the majority of the staff to avoid, almost entirely, any formal debating of the issues. What took place in the eventual staff meetings was more in the nature of professional development than debate.

Developing a policy

During this period I set up the working party agreed to before my sick leave. I decided not to include anyone else from the senior management team in the working party, partly because we had already discussed the issues, and partly because I did not want the suggestions coming from the working party to be seen as imposed from above. I also did not include any of the teachers to whom I was particularly close. I felt that it was crucial that Christine be involved if she wished to be, so asked her and another young teacher (Tina) to join me in the working party. Both agreed and, after some meetings about what we wanted in the discussion document, each of us drafted part of it. After further discussion I put together the whole document.

The discussion document concentrated solely on curriculum areas and did not deal with institutional racism or racist incidents at all since we felt that some staff would react badly to the introduction of these issues at this stage. Curriculum issues seemed safer because they were constantly discussed in the school in other contexts and staff were unlikely to feel personally attacked if they were raised. Racism, on the other hand, was a new issue for discussion and the working party was very much aware of the ways in which some members of staff had taken up, for example, the subject of Brent and the Honeyford case as arguments against developing anti-racist education. We did not want to risk endangering the whole process by *starting* with an area which might raise hackles, although we recognised that dealing with racism was absolutely necessary. The draft document was sent to the Multicultural Adviser and he and I met to discuss it. We agreed that the document should be taken to the staff for discussion and that he would come to the following staff meeting, at which he would raise the issues of racism and, in particular, of racist incidents.

Discussion of the document took place over two staff meetings and initial guidelines for 'Education for a Multicultural Society' were drafted by me in the light of these meetings. These guidelines were brought to the next staff meeting, which the Multicultural Adviser attended. He led the discussion, introducing the issue of racist incidents, as a result of which the staff agreed to the redrafting of the guidelines to include not only ways of dealing with such incidents but also, importantly, a timetable for implementation of the whole policy.

It is interesting to note that, in the period leading up to this meeting, some members of staff persisted in denying the existence of racist incidents in the school or the relevance of anti-racism when we had so few black pupils. Our children, they said, were colour-blind and multicultural or anti-racist education were issues for schools with large numbers of black pupils. However, in the fortnight following the Adviser's visit, every member of staff told me about at least hearing one racist remark or being aware of at least one such incident. Obviously, a change had occurred in their awareness and it was certainly the case that Rose and Sharon, who remained unconvinced, became isolated and any doubt that an anti-racist policy would be put in place disappeared. The initial judgement of the working party, that it would have been counter-productive to raise the issue of racist incidents ourselves was proved correct. The Adviser was able to do so much more effectively, partly because of his status and partly because he was an outsider. Note here the strategic nature of our thinking. While luck, chance, timing and commitment are certainly important, so too is thinking about strategies which are likely to succeed.

When teachers at Bankhead were asked, two years later, to reflect on what had made the most lasting impression on them, nearly all said that it was the dawning realisation of what their black pupils had to endure. The crucial factor in crystallising this realisation was the decision, taken at the suggestion of the Adviser, to monitor racist incidents, for teachers were appalled at the amount of abuse uncovered in a short period amongst children from five upwards.

The relative isolation of the two teachers who still opposed anti-racist initiatives meant that they had, however unwillingly, to take part in the process of monitoring. Once that had begun and the true level of racist incidents began to surface, they became even more isolated, as the waverers became more convinced and opponents changed their minds. By the time I left the school, Rose was the only opponent left and the process had acquired an impetus of its own.

Continuing development

After I left, the school continued to develop its policy and practice. The policy on racist incidents was implemented, allowing the aggrieved child to choose the teacher who would deal with it and to be present for at least part of any discussions with the offender. All such incidents, including those which did not directly involve a black child, were to be recorded. This record book was to be made available at all staff meetings, with specific reference made to it at regular intervals to keep the issues alive. Another important way in which issues of anti-racist education were kept on the agenda of the school was the fact that the Multicultural Adviser continually used it as an example to others when he arranged county-wide in-service training on multicultural and anti-racist education.

In this way teachers at the school and, more particularly, the head gained kudos for having developed anti-racist policy and practice. They gained reward and recognition which validated what had been achieved and helped them progress further. This legitimation is an illustration of the way in which contradictory discourses can operate at one and the same time. In spite of attacks on anti-racism in popular media and national politics, the appointment of the Multicultural Adviser lent weight to 'official counter- discourses' of the time, and he was instrumental in creating validating experiences for those involved in the development of anti-racist education in the county.

As I discovered on a later visit to the school, anti-racist work was undertaken in the taught curriculum which resulted in, for example, some outstanding drama on the issue of imperialism with the Year 6 unit of two classes (that is children aged 10-11). This work started as an exploration of the meaning of the word 'oppression'. Children were divided into two groups, the larger told that they lived in a peaceful, self-sufficient village, and the smaller group who were to be 'explorers and conquerors'. Both groups spent the first session setting up their scenarios, with the 'villagers' working out what they needed in their village, in terms of both material attributes and laws, in order to live peacefully and self-sufficiently. (The children themselves suggested that laws would be necessary.) Meanwhile, the 'conquerors' decided how they would find out if the village was worth conquering and developed a strategy for doing so. Over the next three weeks, the classes spend part of most days working on the drama and writing up the story. Developments were exciting and unpredictable, with the villagers developing strategies of resistance and the conquerors responding with ever increasing repression. Some of the conquerors objected to the repression and went over to the villagers' side, taking with them valuable information. The final sentence of the story, — written as a group story, with wording agreed by the whole class — read 'We think that the most important word in the world is 'freedom''.

By now there seemed to be an increasing move in all the units towards encouraging collaborative group activities amongst the children. These had always played an important part in the education offered to the children at Bankhead. However, with the development of anti-racist work, teachers found that they needed to allow more space and time for children to discuss issues of race with them and amongst themselves as they worked. On revisiting the school, it appeared to me that teachers had become more self-critical in their teaching. They also seemed more open with themselves and their colleagues about any difficulties faced in developing anti-racist strategies, and were eager to address these through discussion in the staff room. As I noted in my diary:

> I spent the day on a visit to [Bankhead] School. I was excited and heartened by some of the staff room discussion going on — and I'm sure not 'put on' for my benefit. Polly and Anne were having a serious discussion about how they should handle a [six-year old] child in their unit who had expressed distaste for the smell of curry while drawing a picture of an Indian after listening to an Indian folk tale. They went carefully through a number of possible approaches — from telling the child they disagreed with him to developing a project on tastes and

64

smells which would be an opportunity for work round science and provide opportunities to challenge prejudices about particular smells and tastes.

Developments were, of course, patchy, with some teachers doing much more than others. I was told that, for some time, Sharon and Rose (who were now part-time and doing a job- share) had continued to resist anti-racist change. However, when I visited the school, even their classroom displays showed evidence of a move away from an anglocentric curriculum, with displays of work on water as one of our human needs showing both African rain masks (taken from a traditional African story) and work on clean and dirty water. This may have been somewhat 'multicultural', but considering that these were two teachers who had, for some time, actively resisted developing multicultural or anti-racist education on the grounds that 'we don't have many of them here', it shows considerable development in the school as a whole.

The role of the head

In reflecting on the process of change in this school, it is, perhaps, significant that it was not led by a strong head with a clear commitment to anti-racist education. Rather, the vacuum created by the absence for some time of a permanent head allowed the space in which it was possible to work for change. Jack's position as the new head, of allowing the process to continue and giving it time and tacit encouragement was significant. It is, perhaps, as important for heads to be willing to allow this space as it is if they lead the development — provided, of course, that there is a movement for change from below, supported and motivated by influential staff. It is, however, essential that heads do not oppose change because they have the power to allow or not allow the time necessary for staff development in the form of staff meetings and, possibly, school- based courses. In addition, heads have the major responsibility for presenting and justifying change to Governors and parents.

It was also significant that, in this particular school, there was a tradition, established consciously by its first head, of having a strong and vociferous staff. This meant that my role in initiating anti-racist change was rendered easier — not because there was not opposition but because teachers at the school were used to discussing educational issues and reflecting on their practice. Members of staff who had been at the school since it opened in 1978 had come to expect this and those appointed later were either appointed because they were expected to fit into this model or came to do so rapidly anyway, because that was the history and tradition of the school.

Then and now

In this case study, it can be seen that the legitimation provided by the Multicultural Adviser played an important part in encouraging and facilitating developments at the school. So the question arises of whether such validation and support would still be possible post-ERA. In some ways, the answer must be that it would be more difficult to obtain. However, many LEAs retain their multicultural or anti-racist policies and many inspectors who were previously multicultural advisers have joined the general inspectorate, which is, in some ways a better position for the advancing of anti-racist education than that of being a multicultural adviser (see Epstein 1991a, chapter 4).

Furthermore, the National Curriculum itself is not monolithic. Both the inclusion of references to the need for equal opportunities in many of the curriculum documents and, in particular, the National Curriculum Council's (NCC) *Guidance on Citizenship* (1990) provide legitimation from within official counter-discourses for the development of anti-racist policies and practices within schools. For example, the *Guidance on Citizenship* states that, in relation to the component of the curriculum dealing with being a citizen:

> Learning about duties, responsibilities and rights is central to this component. Rights include civil, political, social and human rights and how these may be violated by various forms of injustice, inequality and discrimination, *including sexism and racism.*

> (p. 6, emphasis added)

Thus, while the micro-politics of the school will have changed in the context of the ERA, the elements involved in micro-politics — national and local contexts, the history of the school, conflict, persuasion, luck, strategy and so on — will continue to have considerable importance.

2. Badminton Middle School — working as an 'Outsider'

'Badminton' Middle School is a predominantly white school in an affluent suburb of a large industrial city. The head had approached the multicultural support service for assistance in developing multicultural education at the school, following its prioritisation by staff in discussions about their needs for staff development. The project on which I was working agreed that another teacher adviser and myself should provide the help requested.

I came to Badminton Middle School with the experience of change derived from my work at Bankhead School and, although I soon learnt that there were clear differences between being a part of the permanent staff of the school and being an 'outsider' — albeit with the status of teacher adviser — this was important in helping me formulate strategies for working in this new situation. The school, too, was very different. While both had very few black pupils, Bankhead's tradition of 'reflective teaching' (Pollard and Tann 1987) was one which facilitated processes of change. Badminton's tradition, on the other hand, was one of formality and didacticism, which posed altogether different problems in relation to the development of anti-racist teaching at the school.

Initial stages

The concern of the staff about their black pupils had been raised by the deputy head, Dave. He had applied for the DES 1/86 course on *Education for a Multi-Ethnic Society* 'looking for more knowledge about different faiths' and because, as he commented in an interview:

> I felt that being in a predominantly white school, if I wanted to move I .... may well have to move into a school that's predominantly mixed or one ethnic minority group and I felt, for my own personal development, I could do with something.

Thus, by his own account, Dave began the course without any great understanding of or commitment to multicultural or anti-racist education. The course had gradually changed his perceptions of what was necessary. In my interview with him, he described the one session exploring the evidence of discriminatory streaming of black and white pupils as a turning point. Another was his school-based project which had started off as a multi-faith project. But as he was working on it he:

> thought, well, the best thing that I'm going to do is ask the clients, so I thought, well, I'll ask the children what they want, what they feel, how they see the school, and I think that was the biggest eye-opener... we had quite an interesting conversation, a very interesting conversation — things like, what we considered was multicultural assemblies, that some of these children absolutely loathed and detested, because every time we talked about a black person, everybody else in the class assumed it was them ...

67

In the course of his research, Dave interviewed the black children about their experience of schooling, and their replies had startled and surprised him. For example, when he asked them whether they felt 'uncomfortable during any lessons', one of the children commented on:

> pictures of Zulus in books — people take the mickey, [and] assume all black people live like this [and that] only people from Britain or America live in proper houses. ... Sometimes I feel that the teacher means that all black people lived like [jungle tribes] before coming to Britain — and most still do.

He found that the children were also very unhappy about the prevalence of racist jokes and one of the girls remembered vividly 'the first coloured (sic) joke when she was four. It was made by another four year old'.

Dave raised these issues with other members of staff, confronting them with evidence of the black children's perceptions of the school and, largely as a result of his work, multicultural education was the top priority when staff assessed their in-service needs at the end of 1986/7. This did not, of course, mean that all staff were equally committed to or convinced of a need for the development of multicultural/anti-racist education in the school. The head, while not hostile, was acceding to his staff's demands, rather than personally convinced. There were at least two members of staff who were relatively hostile. However, the general feeling was one of goodwill and concern for black pupils in the school, combined with a somewhat stunned recognition that these pupils' experiences of schooling were, to say the least, not always positive.

We began collaborative work at the school at the beginning of the Autumn term of 1987, starting with a series of six weekly in-service training sessions. These sessions dealt with definitions of racism, prejudice and discrimination, institutional racism, thematic approaches to teaching, resources, supporting ethnic minority children in a predominantly white school and school policies. All the sessions allocated time for teachers to discuss in small groups the issues raised, as well as there being some kind of introduction or stimulus from the facilitator and discussion in the whole group.

The sessions appeared to engage the interest and commitment of many of the teachers. However, it was a problem that some of the underlying doubts and even hostility to the aims of the project were never raised within the context of the INSET. A general pattern emerged for all the sessions — unless teachers worked in small groups of two or three, they were dominated by four of the staff, including Harry, the head of the school, and Dave. This meant that Erica the probationary teacher, who supported the philosophy of the project but lacked confidence, and two other teachers, Pam and Maureen, who were doubtful about the whole enterprise, did not raise their concerns 'publicly'.

Their doubts were brought out into the open only in situations in which they felt they were unlikely to be challenged — for example, in informal staffroom discussions with one another, when the normal staffroom 'gripes' were extended by complaints about having to adapt to the project — and in various indirect ways — such as not finding time to prepare work agreed between themselves and the teacher advisers. Failure to do agreed preparation for class teaching and to follow up work done in the classroom sessions had important effects on what was actually achieved with the children in the classes of these teachers. Since we spent only one day a week in each teacher's class, it was critical that preparatory work and follow-up was undertaken by the class teacher — for in its absence the children interpreted what we were doing as a kind of 'bolt on' extra. Furthermore, lack of continuity meant that neither they nor their teachers were able to assimilate or explore further the questions that we raised in our sessions.

Chapter 2 examined the ways in which the positions we hold in discourse can be contradictory, particularly in terms of power relations. We saw that developing ways of combating dominant ideologies is not a simple process. This is further complicated when those engaged in the contest can be seen as being in a position of authority or power. This was certainly the case in the context of our project. As teacher advisers, we had a status that gave us the authority to challenge racism in the schools in which we worked. Indeed this was our stated task. We were seen by members of staff as having more power than they in this particular context, even though we may, at times, have experienced our situation as being one of relative impotence, and both views had a basis in material conditions.

What we were asking of Pam and Maureen was a considerable shift in terms of their classroom practice — and therefore their image of themselves as teachers — and their understandings of racism — and therefore their identities as white women. These shifts were difficult for them, and were not, in my judgement, made during our period at the school.

Part of their resentment was due to the extra work involved, at a time when teachers felt themselves to be very much under pressure and constantly subjected to 'discourses of derision' on the part of New Right politicians and popular media — in fact subject to the kind of marginalisation and derogation often experienced by members of oppressed groups. Add to this the fact that Harry and Dave were both men in senior positions who tended to dominate discussions, while Pam and Maureen were both women in relatively junior positions, and the various subjectivities and relationships become more complicated still. I believe that what was operating between us and these two women was resistance in both a political and psychological sense — that in this case the political was also very much the personal.

A complicating factor in Badminton Middle School was that neither we nor the staff were clear about exactly what we would be doing and trying to achieve in our time there. This was partly because we began with our knowledge of the school based merely on two visits before we actually started working there and partly because of our own inexperience in the project — so that we were not aware of the importance of making clear agreements before work started. One manifestation of the problems created by this omission was that we had to negotiate the very basis of our role in the classroom with each individual teacher. I wrote in my field notes at one stage: that 'I find I'm inadvertently being drawn into being just an extra pair of hands'.

This meant engaging in a delicate renegotiation of roles with the teachers concerned during our second week in the school, and, although this did not become a major problem, it might easily have done so. Moreover, lack of clarity about objectives made it difficult to monitor and evaluate progress. We learnt much from this and we managed matters differently in our next school.

The style of the head and its effects on teaching

Harry was an avowedly authoritarian head, and took this stance with the teachers as well as the children. For example, staff meetings consisted mainly of Harry telling the teachers what was happening and what they were expected to do. There was a subject based timetable to which teachers were expected to adhere and, at the end of each term, each teacher had to submit plans for the following term's work, giving not only an outline of the topics to be covered and the objectives for the term, but also a lesson by lesson plan for each subject area. This meant that it was difficult to allow children's work to develop in unexpected directions.

This authoritarianism was reflected in teachers' handling of the children and of the curriculum, which was lacking in any awareness of either gender or race issues, and allowed no room for flexibility. In most of the classrooms, children sat in desks organised in rows. They were expected to work individually, in silence, from worksheets, the board or books. Teaching was done from the front of the classroom, using talk and chalk and, occasionally, pictures or maps. The only lessons in which the children were expected or allowed to move around, apart from physical education, were art, and craft, design and technology (CDT). Most of the staff had been at the school for many years, and this way of working was thoroughly ingrained. A major part of the collaborative work in Badminton Middle School was, therefore, directed towards trying to shift approaches to teaching away from the very formal towards a more democratic pedagogy.

Other opinion leaders

There were, however, some beginnings of change before we arrived at the school. This was apparently engendered partly by Dave when he was appointed deputy head, who was unhappy with the way the school ran when he started there. Another factor was cuts in staffing, which resulted in teachers keeping their own classes most of the time, instead of teaching subject specialisms in a way closer to a secondary school model. According to Dave, when he started at the school:

It was the Head's view of what a middle school should be and ... he felt that the fourth years were secondary children and should be treated as such. Unfortunately that rubbed off all the way down the school, so that at the age of eight, when the children came in, they almost dropped into the secondary system, and even the eight year olds here might be having three, four or five teachers a week [for] different lessons.

By the time we came to the school, considerable change was already underway. For the most part, teachers kept their own classes and they were about to embark on a trial period of using topic-based approaches to learning. Nonetheless, given that our model for developing anti-racist education rested on ideas about democratising classroom practice, with much co-operative work and an absence of worksheets, it was necessary that a great deal of effort should be expended in exploring these ideas with teachers in the classroom. The teachers had to be convinced that a completely different pedagogy could be employed, as well as undertaking work on issues of inequality. It was clear from the start that the head was not likely to favour such developments in pedagogy, and this was a potential problem, since the influence of the head is of great importance in school change (Ball 1987).

There were other opinion leaders in the school, notably the science teacher, Susan and Olivia, who had been at the school for some twenty years. It became clear during our first weeks in the school that it was to these teachers and the deputy that the other teachers turned for help and support when they ran into problems. Their opinions were influential, both in staff meetings and informal discussions. Dave identified Susan as his most important ally in building up support for making multicultural anti-racist education a high priority for staff and school development. One of the other members of staff said in an interview that she had made multicultural/anti-racist education her highest priority in discussions about staff development because:

> I was completely thrown by what Dave discovered in his school- based project and didn't know what to think about it. I had always thought that Abigail [a black child in her class] had a bit of a chip on her shoulder, but his evidence made me think again. On the other hand, I don't think I would have voted for multicultural education as a priority if Olivia hadn't spoken to me about it and convinced me we should do it. I've got other priorities like art and music which I think we need to look at. But when Olivia spoke to me she persuaded me to change my mind.

It was appropriate to choose to work collaboratively with the 'opinion leaders' first because it would help us with other members of staff if we could influence them. However, because we had no prior knowledge of the school, we did not actually plan this — we had no strategy for identifying them.

Fortunately though, by chance rather than choice, I worked with both Susan and Olivia in our first term at the school.

It is difficult to establish exactly what effect our work with these 'opinion leaders' actually had on the whole school. What was certainly clear was that during the first weeks of our intervention at the school, staff expressed doubt about our approach. For example, my field notes describe an interchange in the staffroom about co-operative teaching as follows:

> Discussion at lunch-time turned on co-operative work by children. Pam expressed the opinion that 'children of this age can't really co-operate. It's as much as they can do to share crayons without arguing'. Maureen agreed, saying that she knew it was 'the current fashion', but, in her opinion, 'children need to be able to work on their own before they can co-operate'. I replied that this was not my experience, but did not pursue the subject.

Towards the end of the term, however, it seemed that staff were more open to ideas about co-operative work, and to allowing children the freedom to talk to each other during lessons. I have argued elsewhere (Epstein and Sealey 1990) and in chapters 6 and 7 of this book, that co-operative work is an essential feature of effective forms of anti-racist pedagogy, as well as being appropriate in terms of children's cognitive development, and there is considerable agreement amongst writers on anti-racist education that this is the case (for example, Francis 1984, Brandt 1986, Lee and Lee with Pearson 1987, Carrington and Short 1989). Consequently, we concentrated heavily on developing co-operative work — amongst both children and staff — especially in the early stages of the project. This did not seem to have an impact on the staff, confirmed by the experiences of those teachers with whom we were working. For example, my diary for 8 November reads:

> Sylvia came into the staffroom very excited about the way in which some of her year five children are managing to co-operate in science lessons. She started talking about it to Erica [their class teacher], who has generally been one of the most anti. By the end of the discussion, Erica was saying (a bit doubtfully) that perhaps she would try some [co-operative work] in her classroom.

That this is linked to the work of the project is confirmed by other observations. Thus, an entry in my research diary for 12 September reads:

> Spent today in observation of the teachers with whom I'm going to work. Most (all?) teaching seems very formal — the only time the children talk is when they answer questions and all the work is done individually. This is a real problem — will have to work hard at developing co-operative work.

However, on 11 October, I wrote:

We seem to be making progress in developing co-operative work. This is particularly noticeable with year seven — both in class and in science lessons — though I'm not sure if it happens when I'm not there. Still, both Oliva and Susan say that they're impressed with how well the children are beginning to work together, in the fourth year at least. Susan still needs convincing that the same approach can work with younger children, but she says she is prepared to give it a go. I am due to have a meeting with her tomorrow to discuss possibilities for group work with years four and five.

Opposition

Some aspects of opposition to the work of the project have been mentioned above. A significant element of opposition came from some of the school's Governors. This became clear at a meeting we had with the governing body in November 1987. My notes on this meeting record that:

> The Governors' meeting was quite an ordeal. ... Most of the Governors did not say anything, but the Secretary and the Chair were very hostile. The Secretary was concerned about 'the poor white children in Handsworth'. Surinder asked what she meant by that and the Chair said that 'there are individual white children in Handsworth schools who experience name-calling and abuse from black children'.

Although two of the Governors, who visited the school and observed members of the project team at work, later came to support the work, the hostility of other Governors created a definite block to the formulation of a school policy against racism.

Others who could be seen as 'blockers' were Pam and Maureen. Fortunately, neither was an opinion leader, but their passive resistance was a problem, especially in our first term at the school. Their opposition did not (often) take the form of arguing a case against what we were doing, Instead, they did no preparation or follow-up work (discussed above), arrived late for in-service sessions and made excuses when we were due to meet with them to plan work — unless the time had been arranged previously with the head and took place during lesson time while he took their classes. Pam's final evaluation of the project in July 1988 reveals both continued subterranean opposition and an attempt to adapt to the demands of the project:

> Personal awareness of my own feelings, ideals and prejudices has become more noticeable. Some pre-1988 ideas have been shattered but a more balanced approach has taken their place. ...

> I have found the Multicultural Input (sic) very valuable and most stimulating. I do however wonder if it would have been so easy to adjust my ideas if we had a higher percentage of coloured (sic) children in our school.

The school visits we made in connection with this work opened my eyes to a multitude of problems, many of which seemed to stem from dispute between Asian and Caribbean (sic) people as well as white people. Is it an ideal that we can all live together with equality and justice? It is very hard to find ways of overcoming built-in prejudice.

A third teacher, Frank, whom we classed as a 'blocker' in the early days of the project, had his own agenda which was largely unrelated to our work. At the start of the project he considerably resented our intervention and, early in the first term, I walked into the staff room just in time to hear him say 'It's much easier to get promoted in this city if you're black'. We dealt with this comment by making sure, in the context of one of the INSET sessions, that we provided information about the very small number of black teachers in Birmingham, especially in promoted posts, and their marginalisation in Section XI posts. However, we found that it was easier to shift his opposition because, in spite of his initial resistance, he was willing to change his practice and, as Lyseight-Jones (1989) says:

> If behaviour changes attitude then the changes which we would wish to focus on will comprise elements which require behavioural change, and, implicit within that, an attitudinal change.
>
> (p. 50)

In practice, Frank found unexpected rewards in changing his behaviour in class. In his final evaluation of the work of the project at the school, he wrote:

> There is a greater interaction between pupils and teacher and the beginnings of more openness is apparent in group and class discussions. There is a greater freedom of expression on my part and similarly on the children's part. ... Through regular full and frank discussions in the staff room there is a greater awareness of what is going on throughout the school. ... The project has certainly altered the way in which an almost all-white school sees its role in meeting the needs of the children in a multicultural, multiracial society. We cannot, and do not, pretend that it does not concern us.

This evaluation of changes in his classroom are confirmed by the observations of another teacher adviser, who commented that 'it's like working with a completely different person'. Shortly after the project finished its period of intervention at the school, Frank left to take up a promoted post in an inner city school. It has not been possible to find out whether he has taken anti-racist practice with him to his new post. However, the change in him over the year was probably the most dramatic — from hostile opponent to strong supporter — even though he may have been, in Lyseight-Jones' terms, a 'bandwagoner'. Here, again, we have an example of contradictory discourses at work. While it may seem unlikely that someone would become a 'bandwagoner' of a 'derided discourse' like anti-racism, the oppositional discourse which had been established in the school through the work of the deputy and the presence of the project, meant that Frank could join the 'bandwagon' in his particular institution.

Evaluations

The intervention at Badminton School was evaluated in a number of ways. My research diary, already referred to, was one. Secondly, I interviewed several of the teachers at the beginning of the project and again some time after its involvement with the school ended. Thirdly, we asked the children themselves to evaluate what they were learning. Fourthly, we had an external evaluator, who, in theory, would visit the school at regular intervals during the project's work there. In practice, she was able to visit the school on only two occasions.

In addition, at the end of the year teachers were asked to fill in an evaluative questionnaire which covered a number of aspects of the project, including its effect on teaching methods and styles. All of them mentioned encouraging more participation from children and engaging in more group work. One fairly typical evaluation, for example, reads:

> [Teaching methods] are much more group-based than previously and include an enormous increase in the use of oral work in group discussion. The children are encouraged to think more for themselves, rather than being 'spoon-fed' from the front. I think that the children are learning to relate more to one another and also to me. I find myself contributing more from within and from my own experiences.

The question remains as to whether such a self- evaluation can be accurate, and whether the use of such methods survived after our intervention ceased. A visit to the school a year after the project's work there ended did reveal that desks were organised in groups rather than rows, allowing the physical possibility of co-operative work without major disruption to classrooms. However, it seemed that collaborative work only took place in 'topic' lessons and, interestingly, in mathematics, while the bulk of teaching time continued to be formal and didactic.

In trying to account for the survival of change in 'topic' work and mathematics, it seems to me that different factors were at work. Thematic approaches were new to the school when the project began its intervention there, so teachers' experience of 'topic' work had been gained in situations where collaborative learning was encouraged. However, since our intervention had been confined to two days a week and consequently to lessons dealing with the chosen topic, other lessons had not changed (or not much) during our presence and teachers saw their themes as a separate 'subject' rather than (as we would have hoped) a way of approaching the whole curriculum in an integrated way. In mathematics, the mathematics advisory team had begun work in the school towards the end of our intervention. Since they too were committed to collaborative teaching and learning, this approach had been strengthened in this area of the curriculum.

However, there does appear to have been a major change in the degree of co-operation between staff in planning, discussing and evaluating work. For example one of the staff to whom I spoke on the return visit said that, 'We are more willing to share our experiences. We admit more readily our worries. Successes and methods are discussed amongst ourselves'. A year later, staff were planning collaboratively for topic work, and appeared to have both formal and informal methods of joint evaluation of work and resources. Regular staff meetings were set aside for planning themes, evaluating resources and evaluating work with children. In addition, several of the staff recounted instances of informal co-operation between themselves continuing. I believe that the co-operation between teachers survived because they found it directly useful and rewarding in planning and evaluating their work.

The teachers all expressed the feeling, at the end of the project, that their understanding of racism was greater and that they would continue to deal with issues raised by the project. However, no policy was established, nor any action plan, which would allow for monitoring and evaluation of progress. This had been one of our initial objectives for the school. However, we were unable to set up any mechanism by which this could be built into the work of the project at the school. This was largely due to our failure to convince the head of the necessity or usefulness of developing a policy. He said that his unwillingness to facilitate the development of policy was due to two factors. Firstly, he said, 'I don't see the need for this. I'm sure the staff will continue to develop multiculture (sic) without a policy' (response to evaluation questionnaire). Secondly, he raised the hostility, discussed above, of several of the school's Governors, including the Chair of Governors, to such an initiative, and indeed to the involvement of the project at the school.

Some time after the Governor's meeting, when the question of setting up a group to look at the possibility of developing a whole school policy arose, Harry expressed the opinion that this would be asking for trouble. 'We had enough problems with the Governors at that meeting and don't want to court more'. In addition to the head's lack of enthusiasm for developing a policy or structures to deal with issues of racism, the opinion leaders amongst the staff could not be convinced that these were a necessary part of anti-racist development in the school. For example, Dave wrote, in response to a question about policy in the final evaluation questionnaire:

> Ethos is the word not structures — once you have changed the ethos of a school then the work flows from this. I don't believe that structures are any use if the staff are not committed to teaching in an anti-racist way.

However, when new staff are appointed it must be made quite clear that if they are not going to teach in this way then they will not be appointed to the school.

It seems that our success in convincing the staff of the importance of pedagogy and of the culture of the school and classroom was used to avoid developing policy. I believe that this was a failure. While policy on its own does not make a school anti-racist in effect (Macdonald 1989), relying on concepts like 'ethos' without the support of a framework within which developments can be monitored, is equally unlikely to be effective. Such concepts are too vague to be evaluated adequately and are subject to considerable variation in interpretation. For example, we saw how most of the teachers at Bankhead were convinced that there was little or no racial abuse taking place in the school until they were asked to monitor racist incidents. Without monitoring and an action plan they were unable to judge the ethos of the school adequately.

Small change

It is perhaps not surprising in the circumstances that there was little evidence, when I revisited the school, that issues of race were being dealt with in the curriculum in any systematic way — although some of the teachers did seem to be taking them up in their classrooms. Neither was it surprising that procedures for dealing with racist incidents were still vague and informal. The only concrete development which Harry could cite to support his claim that there was 'now greater equality of opportunity' in the school, was that two black children had been selected to play the main parts in the school play (which was *Oliver)* and he felt that this would not have happened prior to the project because 'we would have assumed that Oliver and Nancy had to be white'.

It is likely that the relatively minor changes effected in Badminton School were partly a reaction to our asking them to change too much, and all once. One school of thought among anti-racist professionals is that it is better simply to graft on information about issues of race, and, possibly, some degree of multiculturalism, to the existing methods and ethos of the school — and this view was represented on our Steering Committee. However my view, as argued in this book, is that pedagogy is an intrinsic part of successful anti-racist practice in schools, and that it would have defeated the object had we merely attempted to change lesson content. The changes noted in co-operation between teachers and the survival, to some extent, of collaborative work in classrooms were gains, and it is possible that the recent appointment of a new head will allow them to be consolidated and issues of race dealt with in a more substantial way.

Another factor which made change less likely was lack of support from the LEA for developments resulting from the work of the project. Because of pressure on our time we were unable to offer much in the way of continued support to the school after our year there was over; none of the Equal Opportunities Advisers made visits to the school after we had left; and the General Adviser for the school did not regard anti-racism as part of her responsibility. As indicated at the beginning of this chapter, change takes place over time and involves taking risks. In the absence of rewards to counterbalance the risks, it is hardly surprising if movement is slight. Furthermore, the staff at the school had experience of being exposed to adverse publicity at the beginning of our association with it, so they were very much aware of what the risks might be and likely lack of reward. At the end of the project, all the teachers wished for further support. That support would include advisory and liaison involvement, in-service sessions and financial support for more apt materials, and we suggested that discussions between the school, ourselves and the LEA in the form of Equal Opportunities and Schools Advisers should be arranged to facilitate this.

Such discussions never took place and support was not forthcoming. Of course, there is no real answer to the question 'How much support would be enough?' but clearly none is not enough if gains are to be made and sustained.

3. Jennings School — Mixed Responses

Alison Sealey and I worked as teacher advisers at 'Jennings' School, a large primary school in a working class area of the city. It had very few black pupils and several of the classes were entirely white. Jennings was very different to Badminton Middle School. In general, the teachers there considered themselves committed to 'child-centred' approaches and Terry, the head, Joyce the deputy in post when we first visited the school, and one other teacher had all done the DES 1/86 course. Derek, the new deputy took up his post before we actually began collaborative teaching there. Irene, the Infant Co-ordinator had also applied, with the backing of the head, to do this course, but had been turned down by the Schools' Adviser on the grounds that the school had already had more than its fair share of this particular course. Irene was engaged in doing a Diploma in Early Years Education while we were at the school, and planned to do her project assignments on 'the development of multicultural education with young white children'.

Initial stages

My report to the project's Steering Committee on preliminary visits to the school says that:

> It is clear that there is considerable commitment on the part of the senior management of the school and also considerable experience of developing multicultural/anti-racist education. ... Other members of staff whom I met showed varying degrees of interest, ranging from the keen, through the unsure, to one who felt that multicultural education was inappropriate for children in the Early Years. ...

> The head and deputy both reported that the Chair of Governors was very supportive of multicultural anti-racist initiatives. ...

> They were keen that the project should become involved in the school on the basis of collaborative teaching, to help them develop their thinking further and develop a more unified, whole-school approach. The head was particularly keen to develop work with parents as well as children.

Unlike at Badminton School, there was active support for the project from the Chair of Governors as well as from Terry. He had reported to the governing body that the project would be working at the school for a term in order to 'develop further multicultural anti-racist work'. The minutes of this meeting record that 'the Governors welcomed the commitment by the project ... to work at the school next term, and look forward to receiving further reports from the head on this initiative'. So Terry had no need to fear any opposition from the Governors and, for our part, our work was not beset by difficulties over working with teachers worried about lack of support from the head or the Governors.

We had learnt from our work at Badminton that we needed to know much more about the school before starting collaborative work there and that staff needed to know more about us and our expectations and values. Consequently, instead of doing INSET sessions at the same time as we started collaborative work at the school, we ran them the term before. After consultation with Terry and Joyce who, in turn, consulted with staff, we undertook six after-school sessions on:

Definitions and a look at institutional racism;

Using stories to develop anti-racist themes;

Language awareness in monolingual schools;

Supporting ethnic minority children;

Teaching controversial issues; and

A look at whole school approaches.

During the course of the INSET, some teachers appeared to us not to be participating fully, and were, perhaps, engaged in passive resistance. For example, after the session on 'Teaching controversial issues', I wrote in my diary:

> At today's INSET session I felt even more strongly than before that June, Alice and Pat were taking every opportunity to sabotage the session. When I spoke of the need for helping children develop empathy with others they asked for a definition of the word — which I would have thought would have been part of their vocabulary. They chose to work in a group when we asked them to split into 3s or 4s and then proceeded to spend most of the time chatting about everything but the task we had asked them to do — which was to consider what made an issue 'controversial'.

Alison and I thought it possible that one problem was that the presence of the head and deputy stifled open opposition to anti-racism, since they were both known to be strongly committed to anti-racist development in the school, so we asked them to absent themselves from the last session. This did, indeed, enable some teachers to express their negative feelings about the issues and for us to start engaging with them ourselves and also for their colleagues to do so in the context of structured in-service provision. My diary notes on this final session read:

> At today's session neither Terry nor Joyce were present. This was the first time that Alice, June or Pat actually indicated more or less openly that they were unhappy about the project. I felt positive that they had expressed some of their concerns, though not altogether happy that they had been adequately dealt with in the course of the session. Still, at least they are now out in the open, and we can therefore think about

ways of dealing with them next term when we are working in the school.

At the end of the course of INSET sessions we asked teachers to complete a form asking them whether and what kind of collaboration they would like to engage in when we worked at the school the following term and, as a result, chose to teach collaboratively with Derek, Irene, Naomi, the nursery teacher, and Michael, one of the junior teachers.

These teachers were selected because all were able to identify specific areas they wished to work on — for example, Derek wanted to work on playground behaviour, while Naomi was particularly concerned about gender relations and developing links with parents. Also, we had identified these teachers as allies during the INSET sessions, and, particularly since we were only to spend a term at the school, felt it would be more fruitful to work with them than with either the 'blockers' or the 'don't knows'. However, this decision was problematic because it meant we had little contact with several of the teachers in the school and, clearly, some considered the project an irrelevance in a predominantly white school, as was evident from their choosing not to use the resources we had made available to all the staff.

The style of the head

At this time, Terry wrote a memo to all staff explaining whom we would be working with and saying that the teacher advisers:

> have skills and experience, and access to current research, methods and resources which ought to be available for sharing with all of us and not restricted to a small group of staff
>
> As a result I have agreed with them that they will advise and support us in our whole-school topic 'People at Play' by:-
>
> i) Assisting in our detailed planning ...
>
> ii) Assisting with progress meetings throughout the topic.
>
> iii) Offering advice on resources, etc. as required.
>
> iv) Assisting with an open day/exhibition to demonstrate our work to our community/paired schools, etc.
>
> ... It is hoped that this level of support for the school generally, and four colleagues in particular, will help us develop the city's Multicultural, Anti-Racist policy into school action, and will allow us to examine attitudes and classroom processes, and develop our effectiveness as teachers.

Thus there was, from the start, declared support from the head, and also commitment to particular action during the course of the collaboration.

In terms of Ball's classification, Terry could be described as having an interpersonal style of headship, being 'mobile and visible...[with] an emphasis on personal interaction and face-to-face contact between [himself] and his ... staff' (Ball 1987, p. 88). This meant he was easier to work with than the head of Badminton and also that, as mentioned above, disagreements surfaced only occasionally, although he caused some resentment by using a form of patronage to get what he wanted in the school. When for example, it became possible to promote one main scale teacher to an 'A' allowance, he appointed Naomi, one of his supporters, rather than throw the allowance open to applications from other members of staff.[8] This led to the only open revolt while we were at the school, with the disgruntled staff insisting on a staff meeting to discuss the appointment. While the issue did not affect us directly, the unhappiness it engendered did mean that some of the teachers tended to avoid discussion with us, since we were, to some extent, seen as part of the head's 'feudal' apparatus.

Planning the work

At the beginning of our term at the school, we held a meeting with the staff to begin planning for the project on 'People at play'. We used the results of this brainstorming and discussion to draw up a suggested topic web (see Epstein and Sealey 1990, p. 57), which was subsequently agreed by all the staff. In drafting the topic web, we aimed to provide teachers with opportunities — taken from their own ideas — for exploring issues of power, gender and race and the concepts which we had identified as being essential to anti-racist education (Epstein and Sealey 1990, p. 37). For example, looking at advertisements and television programmes provided the chance to explore the concept of stereotyping, as did the work on monsters, witches, 'goodies' and 'baddies' in books and stories. The concept of justice could be explored through considering 'playing fair', as well as competition. We felt that dealing with racism itself would arise out of work on the playground; on gangs; on football violence; on stories; and would result from work on stereotyping and justice. As part of the planning process, teachers were also asked to complete a checklist for features of anti-racist teaching which asked:

How can I develop aspects of this theme which will:

> use multicultural examples and resources;

> depict people from a range of societies and backgrounds;

> involve the wider community from outside the school walls;

> offer opportunities for children to depict bias;

> help children to recognise and challenge stereotypes;

allow children to direct their own learning, follow their own interests, use 'real' information;

encourage expression of children's opinions [and feelings], sensitively confront negative attitudes;

encourage co-operation, group work, talk;

develop social skills, self-awareness;

develop concepts of justice, fairness, conflict resolution;

expect, facilitate and value high standards of achievement from all children;

explore global issues and interdependence.

(Epstein and Sealey 1990, p. 58)

The following week we had a day conference with the four teachers involved in the collaborative teaching and the head, to draw up individual contracts which we, the particular teachers involved and the head would sign. We had learnt from our experience at Badminton School that we had to establish that we and the staff clearly understood the aims of the project, and to have stated objectives, so that we could monitor the school's project against them. We kept copies of the contracts and so did the head and the teachers. The general contract specified the names of the teachers, the period and days of the collaboration, the roles and forms of facilitation and support to be undertaken by the head. It set out the following objectives for development of the school, staff and pupils:

School:

Whole school policy.

Detailed guidelines in curriculum areas.

Improving communication with parents by involving them more in the life of the school, creating a dialogue to counter negative attitudes and build on positive relationships.

Development of an awareness throughout the school of Jennings as part of the city[9] — e.g. extending links with schools in the inner city in mutually supportive ways.

Development of links with other agencies, particularly for building up resources.

Staff:

Support for all staff in development and implementation of policy and guidelines.

83

Opportunities for regular meetings between all staff to discuss the issues frankly.

Through the above, the development of confidence on the part of all staff to maintain and develop multicultural anti-racist education in future.

Pupils:

Through the development of classroom activities which give pupils responsibility in their own learning, to help pupils develop self-aware-ness and self-esteem. From this foundation, to help them develop empathy and understanding with people in different situations from their own.

Helping children to consider and question their own attitudes, especially about race and gender.

Helping children to understand global issues, e.g. about famine, aid, [etc].

There were also specific contracts between us and each teacher, which outlined what each hoped to have gained or achieved by the end of the project for the school as a whole, for themselves and for pupil groups, together with an outline plan of intended development and starting points in each class. In addition, we made agreements on the frequency and duration of collabora-tive sessions and the roles of the teacher adviser involved and the teacher in the areas of review and preparation, collaborative teaching and evaluation.

Evaluations

All this preliminary work meant that we were much clearer this time about exactly what our aims and roles were to be. It also meant that we and the teachers were in a better position to evaluate the work we did together. At the end of the term during which we worked at the school, we asked the head and the staff with whom we had taught to complete evaluation sheets, which covered the objectives set in the contracts and asked them to comment on tangible achievements, their own perceptions about the development which had taken place, practical possibilities for future development and any short-comings, failures or omissions. All the teachers commented on the success of having children work collaboratively and take responsibility for their own learning. For example, Irene wrote in her final evaluation, 'I was able to see ways in which children can be empowered to make their own decisions'.

This perception came to full fruition a year later, when Irene telephoned me to say that she had been having a great deal of difficulty with her class, which included a number of very aggressive boys:

It came to a head when I had two bloody noses on one day. I thought to myself, 'what would Debbie have done', and sat them down in a circle to have a discussion about how we should handle the situation. The children were amazing — they made really sensible suggestions. Since then we've been playing lots of co-operation games and using circle discussions to decide how to manage conflicts between the children. It's made all the difference.

Derek, who was teaching Year 6, wrote in his final evaluation:

There is a superior quality of discussion and debate in the classroom. By this, I mean the children appear to listen to each other. They use a more appropriate vocabulary and most importantly, are prepared to give their own opinions and experiences. The class seem to accept group work as normal and as a result work well when so arranged.

There does, indeed, seem to have been a change in the children's attitude to offering their opinions in class. For example, early in the term, when Alison asked one of the Year 6 children whether he had something to say because he was talking during the showing of a video of the class at play, he responded by saying 'No Miss' as if he was being told off, although he was, in fact, being asked a genuine question. By the end of the term, this child was willing to participate fully in a discussion on inclusion and exclusion and the possible racist nature of exclusions.

On the other hand, all the evaluations by teachers with whom we collaborated expressed the opinion that the teachers not directly involved in collaboration had gained little from the presence of the project. This was partly a problem of time and partly of communication. The physical design of the school, with separate staffrooms for junior, infant and nursery staff, and two buildings separated by the playground meant that adequate communication, and therefore dissemination of the work of the project, was difficult to achieve. We tried to overcome this by setting up working groups, dealing with different aspects of school experience, to draw up a draft policy statement.

Continuing Development

Each working group was convened by one of the teachers with whom we worked, and they continued after we left the school. The working party eventually did produce a wide-ranging and unusual policy, which, as well as a general statement of intent, covered classroom organisation for equal opportunities, anti-sexism, anti-racism, the playground, resources, parents and community links and assemblies. The influence of the project is clearly visible in the preamble to the section on classroom organisation:

It is important to adopt a whole-school, cross-curricular approach to issues of equality, seeking to move beyond a tolerance promoting,

85

pluralist approach, to an equality promoting, anti-racist and anti-sexist approach which requires us to examine our own attitudes and practices. 'How' children learn is as important as 'What' they learn in determining their attitudes to themselves and to other groups in society. Children should be given a measure of responsibility for how they organise their learning, appropriate to their age, and should have opportunities to express their own views and consider the views of others.

This is followed by a summary of the knowledge, skills and attitudes which teachers should seek to develop in their pupils, including clear recognition of inequalities in the following terms:

Knowledge

Groups may have very different experiences in life, and their ability to secure change may vary;

Skills

The ability to seek change through social and political actions;

Attitudes

To develop a sense of fairness, and be unwilling to accept unsound generalisations;

To see social change as an enrichment, not a threat.

The production of such a policy in itself reflects considerable steps on the part of the school. However, it would certainly have been stronger had it been accompanied by an action plan, setting dates by which certain actions would be taken. Without such an action plan, monitoring the policy's effects was almost impossible.

When I interviewed him two years later Terry was much more concerned to talk about the problems raised by LMS than about developments in education for equality in the school. The external pressures of the National Curriculum and LMS were such that he seemed to have lost sight of much of our work with the school and it is significant that he did not mention the policy, even though I asked him what concrete developments there had been at the school since we had left.[10] This is surely an indication that the policy did not play an active part in his life in the school and one is left wondering how significant it could therefore be in the life of other members of staff or the children. That such deprioritisation of equality issues seems to be a feature of life under ERA has been confirmed by other researchers (for example, Gold et al 1990, Ball personal communication 1991).

Nonetheless, when I made this visit, I could see signs that the kind of work developed by the project was continuing. Such signs can provide a more accurate evaluation of the impact of the project than relying on what teachers say in interviews. Displays of children's work can be a good indicator of the ethos of the school. Where interviews and observation are in accord, the evidence is likely to be reliable.

On one wall, for example, was work on the 'Land of Conformatron', an imaginary country where everyone conformed and behaved in the same way, done by a class whose teacher who had not been directly involved in the collaborative teaching, . Elsewhere there was a display of children's work on 'Making our own decisions'. The nursery had developed a book of nursery rhymes in which traditional rhymes had been altered to avoid sexism and racism, and Naomi told me that these had been discussed with the children, who had, themselves, made some of the suggestions, and that the book was given to visiting adults who came in to work with children, if they were reading them nursery rhymes. She also said that they did drama with the children two or three times a week, and that this often took the form of changing stories which they had read to the children in class. This was a direct result of work with the children and involved them in developing different gender roles for story characters and thinking about ways in which the story might be different if located in a different context.

When asked about planning for the National Curriculum, both Derek and Michael said that the school was doing so within the framework of thematic anti-oppressive approaches to teaching and that when planning themes they took into account the controversial issues raised. For example in a theme on food, which included a visit to a farm, Derek had done work with the children on issues raised by factory farming and surplus and famine which, he said, he would not have thought of doing prior to the project's work at the school.

Cause for concern — and some hope

Despite Terry's undoubted commitment to developing anti-racist education in his school, he became overwhelmed in 1990 by the demands of LMS and the National Curriculum. He found it almost impossible, at this point, to answer questions about progress on anti-racist policies and practices, without embarking on a description of his problems and stresses. The impact of national politics — especially post-ERA and following a fourth Conservative election victory — should not be underestimated and it may well become increasingly difficult in the future to find the time or space for the development of anti-discriminatory policies and practices.

Nevertheless, I believe that there is room for some hope. The developments at Jennings School after we left took place when teachers were having to deal with new initiatives and curriculum documents almost weekly, as well as with the uncertainty engendered by LMS. The fact that the work described above took place in the face of these difficulties and that National Curriculum planning had not prevented thinking about equality issues is, in itself, positive. As we saw earlier, some of the National Curriculum documents hold openings for anti-racist work, and it is these that will have to be developed.

References for Chapter 5

1. However it is not always clear whether, by 'effectiveness' these authors mean the academic achievement of pupils, the social cohesion of the school or some combination of the two. Ball (1990) draws attention to the 'ideological work done by effectiveness improvement' in 'construct[ing] a concept of the ineffective or sick school ' (pp. 89-90).

2. This phrase is taken from Ball (1987, pp. 268-270)

3. This is not to say that such an approach would not be effective in secondary schools. However, I have no experience of working for change in secondary schools and therefore no evidence to back this up.

4. In 1986 the CRE's report on the withdrawal of pupils for English language support in Calderdale constituted indirect discrimination, since withdrawal meant that they missed out on much of the school curriculum and were consequently educationally disadvantaged.

5. I am grateful to Stephen Ball for pointing this out to me, although luck and chance are not issues which he raises in *The Micro-Politics of the School* (1987).

6. Troyna and Carrington (1990, pp. 119-120) point out the importance of mobilising parental support.

7. Ball also discusses the use of interpersonal styles of management in secondary schools (pp. 88-95).

8. This should not be taken to indicate that she did not deserve the post. Naomi was a talented teacher who worked hard and took a lot of responsibility. What is at issue here is the method of appointment.

9. One of the issues raised at the day conference was the 'island mentality' of the school, as a predominantly white school in a multiracial city.

10. Although he did talk of the inclusion of equal opportunities in the School Development Plan undertaken by all schools in the LEA at the introduction of the National Curriculum and Local Management of Schools (LMS).

CHAPTER SIX

'CHILD-CENTRED' AND ANTI-RACIST EDUCATION

'Child-centred' education

Introduction

This chapter starts with a discussion of the origins and influence of ideas about child-centred education, particularly those based on Piaget's work on child development. These ideas, it is argued, were culturally constructed and derived from the positivist tradition of the European Enlightenment. The individualism of this intellectual tradition has led to psychologists and educationists looking at children purely as individuals, isolated from their social context. This is the society/individual dichotomy, discussed in Chapter 2, writ large — for if adults are seen as in some way separate from society, childhood is constructed as some kind of safe vacuum, where children are 'prepared' to take their place in society.

Origins and influence

'Child-centred' education did not spring full-grown from the Plowden Report in 1967. Its origins lie back in the eighteenth century when Rousseau (1762) suggested that human beings 'naturally' develop in certain ways unless prevented from so doing. Philosophies of education deriving in part from Rousseau's views were developed by such late nineteenth and early twentieth century pioneers of early childhood education as Froebel, Montessori and Steiner (Dearden 1968, Bruce 1987). The ideas of these innovators have remained important, especially in early years education, until the present day and have formed part of the basis for the development of 'child-centred' education.

However, one of the chief influences on the development of child-centred education in post-war Britain was Piaget's study of the cognitive development of young children. It is not my intention to summarise Piaget's work

89

here[1] — more important for my purposes than his actual work have been the interpretations of it used in the training of teachers and in classroom practice. The key points in this regard have been Piaget's view of children as 'little scientists' who make their own discoveries about the world — the role of the teacher being to provide the wherewithal for the making of such 'discoveries' and to observe what stage the child has reached;[2] the belief that the way children think is qualitatively different from the way adults think; the notion that young children are unable to decentre and are thus unable to empathise with the points of view of others; the idea that children go through definite and discrete stages in the development of cognition; and the view that such stages will unfold automatically, but can be encouraged by appropriate nurture and stimulus.

It should be noted here that Piaget did not, himself, talk of 'discovery' methods of teaching and learning. Indeed he did not discuss pedagogy at all. However his findings have been taken to imply the need for such 'discovery' methods in mainstream primary teacher education in England. Perhaps Piaget's most important contribution was his belief that children's cognitive development was a result of an interaction between the child and the environment — which opened the way for the later development of social constructionism. However he did not include the social or cultural context as being part of the 'environment'. His focus was very much on individual development and cognition as in his famous experiments on the concept of conservation and his work with Inhelder on moral thinking. By 'interaction between child and environment', Piaget meant an interaction between the children's 'natural' propensities and stages of development (which were seen in biological terms) and their concrete experiences.[3]

This view of child development lies within the positivist and individual-istic tradition of the Enlightenment — with its emphasis on the rational, cognitive and sequential individual. As such, it was a view which fitted well with ideologies and forms of social organisation which had arisen during the development of industrial capitalism, in particular the rise of 'science' as a major form of legitimation (Walkerdine 1984, 1990). The very idea that childhood is qualitatively different from adulthood is culturally constructed and it is only in the last hundred years and in Western industrial countries that this notion has come to be regarded as so obvious that it is regarded as merely 'common-sense'.

Piaget's work has greatly influenced our ideas about child development and appropriate pedagogies for young children. It shifted opinion away from both the view that children's development is completely predetermined by biology and the view that children are, essentially, empty vessels to be filled up with knowledge by adults, towards a more 'interactionist' approach which sees child development as the result of interaction between child and environment (Bruce 1987, pp. 3-8). It also played a leading part in stimulating research about how children think and learn, both amongst those who wished to develop Piaget's ideas and those who were more critical of them.

However from the point of view of the development of English primary education, the most important contribution made by the work of Piaget was its role as theoretical underpinning of the Plowden Report (Central Advisory Council for Education 1967). While it is not clear historically how much the Plowden Committee relied directly on readings of Piaget, their findings and philosophy are clearly consonant with a Piagetian view of child development. The Plowden Report relies on many of the ideas developed by Piaget. Important amongst these are notions about the 'naturalness' of childhood, of sequential development and 'readiness' or, in Plowden's words, 'sensitive periods'. These ideas, at the heart of the Report, led to recommendations by Plowden concerning the organisation of classrooms and the importance of play — ideas which have informed the ideology of primary practice, especially in the Early Years of schooling, since the early 1970s.

It would be easy to exaggerate the implementation of Plowden in practice — studies have found that typical primary classrooms are not, nor have been, organised for learning through exploration, discovery and play (Galton et al 1980, Edwards and Mercer 1987, Tizard et al 1988). Nevertheless, the Plowdenesque ideas of 'discovery learning' and 'stages of development' have played an important part in shaping how we think of primary education.

One result of the individual constructivist perspectives of Plowden is that much educational research has concentrated on theories of learning at the expense of considering approaches to pedagogy.[4] What has been considered important has been understanding the stages of development that children reach at various times — but the fact that there *are* discrete stages has, until relatively recently, been taken as read.[5] The deep-rootedness of this idea can be seen in the fact that, while self-direction of learning by children (which has been relatively rare in practice in schools) has been under attack from the Right, the National Curriculum with its set attainment targets is totally in line with notions of sequential stages of development.

From the point of view of developing education for equality, the discourse engendered by the Plowden Report has been problematic for a number of reasons. Firstly, the wide acceptance of the idea that child development follows discrete and sequential paths and the notion that children cannot decentre until they reach a 'mental age' of ten or eleven has meant that teachers have found it difficult to accept (or easy to reject) the idea that primary age children can handle concepts of racism and sexism. Although the Plowden Committee did not deal with questions of race or gender, the failure to do so by many teachers who regard themselves as being 'child-centred' and in the Plowden tradition, is not an inevitable consequence of the Plowden Report. Nevertheless the notion that children cannot decentre until the secondary phase sits easily with the conviction that they cannot deal with political ideas or thinking about people in situations other than their own — and therefore with the idea that issues of racism and sexism are not appropriately handled in the primary classroom.

91

Secondly, the view of Plowden that children should be seen as individuals rather than as members of groups and the pathologising of social groups when they *are* mentioned, has meant that it has been difficult to raise questions of power relationships in primary schools. This individualistic view is implicit and taken for granted in the Plowden Report. Plowden's heavy stress on individual development and the need to see children as individuals almost precludes acknowledgement of their social position. Again, this is not an inevitable result of considering children as individuals. It is clearly possible to recognise both the individuality of children and the way they are situated within and constitute society. Nevertheless, political and ideological factors — which have tended to favour disregarding social aspects of education — and the individualism of the Plowden discourse have been combined. The outcome is that it is only with the advent of feminism in the 1970s and anti-racism in the 1980s that children have begun to be considered as members of society.

Thirdly, Plowden's deficit view of working-class children has meant that efforts to equalise opportunity have been focused on repairing the deficiencies of individual children rather than on structures and curriculum. This view, similar to that underlying contemporaneous American programmes of compensatory education such as Headstart, is implicit in Plowden's discussion of inequality. The pathologising of working- class 'under-achievement' is a serious flaw in Plowden. Furthermore, the Plowden Report is open to the criticism that, by virtually ignoring issues of race and gender, it tends to be based on the experience of white boys. Deficit and individualised views of black boys and girls and white girls fitted well with its interpretation of class inequality in education.

The Plowden Report contains two different and contradictory views about the relationship between children and society. Society is treated, on the one hand, as an entity from which children must be protected or for which they must be compensated by schools (as in EPAs) and, on the other, as something which children will enter at some future date and for which they must be moulded. Thus, in answer to its own question:

> What agreement can be reached in the midst of this uncertainty about the objectives of ... English primary schools in the last third of the twentieth century?

the Plowden Report replies that:

> one obvious purpose is to fit children for the society into which they will grow up.

> (Central Advisory Council for Education 1967, para. 496)

Both these views were aspects of Plowden discourses which diminished the likelihood that primary teachers working within their framework would try to consider and challenge social inequalities with the children they teach —

for if the school is regarded as a safe haven from the ills of society, why allow disruptive ideas about inequality to enter the classroom? Furthermore, while 'preparing' children to take their place in society (at some unspecified future date) might involve some ideas of liberal tolerance — as it does in the National Curriculum Council's *Guidance on Citizenship* (NCC 1990) — it also carries the implicit assumption that the 'nature' of society is fixed and that we can predict what kind of society children should be being prepared for. Again, there is no compelling logic which says that predictions about a future society will not involve recognition of a need to combat inequalities but the notion does preclude the idea that children should be involved, in the here and now, in deconstruction of dominant ideologies — which I take to be an essential part of an effective anti-racist pedagogy.

The discourse of 'child-centred' education, as expressed in the Plowden Report, has been the subject of criticism from at least two differing viewpoints. Firstly, psychologists interested in child development have raised questions about the validity of Piaget's work, on which much of Plowden's thinking is based. Secondly, criticisms have been made by those interested in the construction of ideologies and power relations within society.

Critiques by developmental psychologists

A number of developmental psychologists have been critical of Piaget's methodology and theories (Bruner 1968a and b, Davies 1991, Donaldson 1978, Hughes, 1975 & 1986, Wood 1988). Donaldson (1978), for example, though acknowledging an indebtedness to Piaget (p. 9) offers detailed criticism of his methodology, pointing out that Piaget's stress on the child as individual prevented him from taking into account the way in which the context of a task affects a child's attempts to tackle it. Donaldson labels this idea 'embeddedness' and describes experiments in which the results of Piaget's classic experiments on conservation and the ability to decentre can be altered by the way in which they are presented to children (Hughes 1975, Donaldson 1978, pp 20-24).

Later work (see, for example, Dunn 1988) has shown conclusively that children as early as their second year — when studied in naturalistic settings — are aware of the feelings of others; they can both comfort those who are distressed and exploit the power of knowing how to justify themselves or how to annoy and upset others. Such awareness of other people's thoughts and feelings is, in my view, a key element in the construction of anti-racist understandings. One justification for not attempting to develop anti-racist strategies in primary schools (and especially in predominantly white ones) has been that, since young children cannot decentre, they are unable to understand political, social or moral issues. However, if it is the case that children as young as two are perfectly capable of decentring, then, *a priori*, they will still be able to do so at five and later — unless, perhaps , they are discouraged from doing so by the constant assumption that it is not possible. Dunn's findings are extremely significant, for they establish empirically that very young children can and do think about the points of view of others, about social and moral issues and about relationships. She shows children understanding and using arguments concerning dominant ideologies — albeit often to justify themselves and in ways which reconstruct rather than deconstruct such cultural expectations. For example, in one interchange reported by Dunn, a child of 36 months (C) uses gender roles to justify to her mother (M) her refusal to allow her brother to play with her toy vacuum cleaner:

M to C: Are you going to let David have a turn?

C to M: I have to do it. *Ladies* do it.

M to C: Yes, ladies do it. Yes, and men do it sometimes. Daddy sometimes does the hoovering, doesn't he?

C to M: But I do it sometimes.

M to C: Yes, but Daddy does it sometimes so you let David do it.

(p. 57, original emphasis)

My own work with young children in schools confirms Dunn's findings, and shows young children able not only to understand, use and construct dominant ideologies, but also to decentre and take part in deconstruction of these same ideologies.6 Observation of children in home and school situations also shows them considering moral issues in some depth. For example, in the following conversation two children, aged four (D) and seven (P), explore the ethics of obedience:

P: Should you always obey an adult?

D: um? Obey ..

P: What if an adult tells you to do something bad? What if Rona [P's mother] told you to do something bad?

D: Well, if *Rona* told me, she very likely wouldn't mean it.

P   Obey or disobey?

(Epstein and Sealey 1990, p. 35)[7]

Similarly Paley's (1987) book, *Wally's stories,* abounds with transcriptions of children in an American kindergarten class seriously discussing complicated moral and political issues.

Critiques of 'child-centred' ideology

Alexander (1984) identifies two characteristics of what he calls the 'primary ideology' (cited in Short 1988, p.11). Firstly, children are thought to be innocent and 'whilst capable of unacceptable behaviour, [they] remain free from malicious intent' (*ibid,* p. 11). Secondly, there is the powerful notion of 'sequential developmentalism' derived from Piaget and discussed above. Both of these aspects of the discourse of primary education militate against possibilities of dealing with controversial issues in primary schools.

Stone (1981) concentrates on criticising the idea that 'self-concept' is an important factor in the underachievement of black children in schools. While not actually using the term 'child-centred education' in her critique, her discussion of 'self-concept' and the danger of teaching based on relationships constitute an implicit criticism. She concludes her book with the statement that:

> ... self-concept research and theory and teaching styles based on these ideas have little to contribute towards an understanding of how West Indian children in Britain should be educated, and may have contributed towards the low attainment of such children — because they stress affective goals of self-expression, self- fulfilment, happiness and so on as the basis of their teaching methods.

> (pp. 253-4)

Stone's work was an intervention made at a particular historical moment in the development of anti-racist/multicultural education, when a dominant theme in education for equality was, indeed, around notions of self-concept — the idea being that black pupils and girls underachieved as a result of poor self-image. Stone had good reason to be critical of such ideas, with their focus on individual black children and their assumed cultures. She comments, for example, on criticisms by Yvonne Colleymore of a Home Economics curriculum which did not include information about hair care and make-up for African-Caribbean girls in the following terms:

> Would the English girls find a Home Economics class on Afro hair care more relevant? Or does it matter? Why should schools have to teach young women how to look after their hair?

> (p. 70)

Stone follows this up by questioning the notion that 'black children as a whole have significantly poor self-concepts' (p. 71) or that self-concept is significant in accounting for relatively 'low achievement' by black children.

However Stone does not appear to take into account the fact that initiatives such as those she describes (for all the sexism in the example quoted) represented a real advance by putting racism on the agenda as an issue for education and, in many cases, arose from the work of black political activists. Bernard Coard (1971), for example, argued precisely that black children had poor self-concept and consequently underachieved as a result of non-acknowledgement of their histories and cultures within the English education system. Furthermore, Stone fails to question the success of formal pedagogies and those which do not take account of children's 'cultures' and histories. It was, indeed, this very failure which led to the writing of Coard's pamphlet and — taken together with the policy of 'bussing' black children to schools outside their home localities — to the establishment of the Black Parents' Movement in 1975 (John 1986). Stone's solution to the problem of 'black underachievement' is a return to formal didacticism:

> ... the central recommendation of this study is for the use of more formal methods of teaching West Indian children throughout primary and secondary schools. ... in the light of the dismal failure of the present approach, *formal teaching methods can only offer an improvement on the present situation.*

(op cit, p. 242, emphasis added)

The implication of this statement is that formal methods have been in the past, and would be in the future, successful in helping black and working class pupils reach the same levels of academic success as middle class white students.

Notwithstanding the work of Neville Bennett (1976), which suggested that children achieved more academically in formal than informal teaching situations, there is little or no evidence that this is so. Bennett's methodology and interpretation of statistical data have been widely criticised[8] and Bennett himself was involved, with Aitkin and others, in a re-evaluation of the original research using different methods of statistical analysis, which found that previously asserted differences in the academic achievement of children taught formally and informally disappeared (Aitkin et al 1981; Gray and Satterly 1981). If it were the case that formal methods of teaching were of benefit to black, female and working class students then one would expect to find, for example, that such groups achieved more academic success in secondary schools — which tend to remain formal in their teaching — than in primary schools. In fact this is not the case. Though some secondary schools show evidence of greater 'school effect' than others, this has not been linked to formal teaching methods but to other factors such as having clear aims (Smith & Tomlinson 1990).

A completely different critique of child-centred education has also been made from a post-Foucauldian perspective — notably by Walkerdine (1981, 1984, 1989, 1990), who has argued that:

> Although [child-centred education] has been widely associated with progressivism and hailed as freeing and liberating children from the authoritarianism of 'chalk-and-talk' methods, it can, in fact, be viewed quite differently. It can be argued that the shift has been not from authoritarianism to liberation, nor from power to no power, but from overt disciplining to covert disciplining, in which 'scientific pedagogy' plays a major role

(1989, p. 21)

In her paper 'Sex, power and pedagogy' (1981), Walkerdine quotes a transcript of a conversation between three nursery school children, in which the boys use sexually abusive language both to a girl class-mate and towards the teacher. In her discussion of this transcript, Walkerdine suggests that these boys have power over their female teachers 'through constituting her as the powerless object of sexist discourse' (p. 15). She sees this as a way in which boys are able to resist their powerlessness as pupils:

> Since the boys are both children and male, and the teacher is both teacher and female they can enter as subjects into a variety of discourses, some of which render them powerful and some of which render them powerless. It is important to note the way in which the boys refer to the teacher and to the 3-year-old girl, Annie, in the same terms. They call Annie a 'cunt'. In this way they bring their teacher down to size: she and a small girl are in discourse but the same thing - sex objects. ... The issue which I have raised would appear to have important consequences for practice. In this example we can understand the boys as both subjects in patriarchal discourse perpetrating patriarchal oppression upon their teacher and at the same time children oppressed/controlled by the authority of the teacher.

(p. 16)

Walkerdine goes on to suggest that the terms of child-centred pedagogic discourse allow children to develop their power in ways which are potentially oppressive to female pupils and teachers:

> ... the very discourse helps to produce the children as powerful. The space is already there for their resistance. ... Since, if [the teacher] reads [the boys'] actions as normal and natural ... she is forced into a no-choice situation. She cannot but allow them to continue ... The very practice which is supposed to liberate ('progressive education'), produces the possibility of this discursive power in the children. There is no counter discourse and the children know it ...

(p. 18)

In relation to Walkerdine's particular example, her strictures carry considerable weight. However, being 'child-centred' does not necessarily entail 'reading the boys' actions as normal and natural'. It would have been possible for the teacher, 'Miss Baxter', to have handled such an incident very differently, while still engaging in (a rather different) form of 'child-centred' education — one which recognises children as active agents in the construction and reconstruction of dominant ideologies and calls upon them to engage in a deconstructive process, using collaborative approaches in democratised classrooms. Examples of such approaches are suggested in the next chapter.

97

Walkerdine relates her critique to class (see, particularly, Walkerdine and Lucey 1989) and gender, but it could equally well be applied in relation to race. If children's expressions of racism (even where they are not fully understood by the children themselves) are left uncountered and unchallenged, then the very act of refraining from challenge legitimates racial prejudice and discrimination. However, I would argue that it is due to the liberal and individualistic framework within which child-centred education has developed that it is open to these strictures and that how the term is interpreted is contingent upon particular political and demographic contexts.

Just as other terms — such as, for example, the 'right to choose' — have been appropriated and reappropriated by the Left and Right respectively, it would be possible for radical educators to reappropriate the term 'child-centred' education, giving it a more political and oppositional content. Just as there is no necessary logical connection between the Plowden discourse and a failure to consider social and political inequalities in education, so too is there no necessity for 'child' or 'student-centred' learning to remain within the framework of liberal rationalism. Indeed, recent writers (for example, Carrington and Short 1989, Cohen 1989, Grugeon and Woods 1990) who have described attempts to develop anti-racist pedagogies which take on board objections to child-centred education have all used teaching methods which 'start where the children are' and are 'person-centred' rather than 'knowledge-centred', while, at the same time holding firm to a view of children as being part of society and therefore involved in the construction and reconstruction of inequalities.

It is unsatisfactory to leave matters at the level of critique, and Walkerdine's work — because it makes no attempt at concrete suggestions about possible ways forward — leaves the reader wondering whether the only solution she sees to problematic aspects of current discourses of 'child-centred' education is a return to formal didacticism. In this book, I have drawn on critiques of child-centred education by Walkerdine and others, while at the same time trying to hold on to the space given by child-centredness for the development of oppositional pedagogy. The argument for doing so will be further developed through case studies of work with children in the next chapter. In doing so, I have built on social constructionist ideas about child development, which will be discussed in more detail towards the end of this chapter.

Approaches to 'racialised' education[9]

Few writers about anti-racist or multicultural education have concerned themselves with pedagogy. In most of the anti-racist literature the emphasis has been on curriculum content (see, for example, Straker-Welds 1984, Arora & Duncan 1986) or on school and LEA policies (for example, Troyna & Williams 1986; various articles in Tierney 1982), but the two areas of research have been largely kept separate from each other. Even in collections where both are addressed by separate authors, explicit linkages are sparse indeed. While work has been done on various aspects of racism in education, the articulations between them have been almost invisible.

'Racialised education' within the child-centred tradition

Among the earliest attempts to 'teach about race relations' was that undertaken as an extension to the Schools Council Humanities Curriculum Project (Stenhouse et al 1982). While this Project was based in secondary, not primary, schools, it falls broadly within the tradition of child-centred education. It was, perhaps, partly for this reason that the members of the team decided to adopt as one strategy[10] the 'neutral chair' approach. Stenhouse et al. (1982) claim that:

> ... the procedural neutrality of the teacher as chairman (sic) rests on the premise that he (sic) is not personally neutral. He adopts a procedural neutrality to avoid asserting his views with the authority of his position behind him. He is likely to adopt the stance of neutral chairman because he believes that it furthers discussion as a search for truth and avoids the shaping of view by mere conformity or rebellion.

> (p. 5)

Stenhouse's approach has its theoretical base in a form of liberal pluralism which lacks an analysis of power relations within society (or the classroom). The framework adopted allows Stenhouse to believe that 'procedural neutrality' is, indeed, possible. He is wrong on a number of counts. Firstly, even very young children — let alone the 15- to 16-year-olds with whom the Humanities Project dealt — are very much aware of teachers' (and other adults') positions and opinions. Moreover, as the Schools Council Project in Moral Education found, students:

> ... expected adults to 'come off the fence', to be willing to reveal their views when asked. Adolescents in a survey claimed, and we believed they were right, that to refuse to state what you think about an issue while expecting others to do so is to adopt a superior position in which you treat others as less than persons.

> (McPhail et al 1972, p. 89)

I would agree it is essential that teachers should be open, in the sense that, as Hall (1980) points out, it is necessary for racist (and sexist and heterosexist) opinions to be articulated in order to allow the possibility of engaging with them. There is however a difference between allowing opinions to surface and legitimating them through a so-called 'neutrality'.

Harwood (1986, p. 52, cited in Carrington and Troyna 1988, p.3) has identified a number of possible approaches to dealing with controversial political issues in the classroom, ranging from the 'committed' role in which the 'teacher is free to propagate her own view on controversial political

99

issues' through the 'impartial chairperson' role to the 'declared interest' role, in which the 'teacher begins by declaring her own viewpoint, so that pupils can better judge bias later' and 'then presents all available positions as objectively as possible'. A variant on this would be for the teacher to declare her viewpoint in a way which does not preclude disagreement, and invite the views of students, asking them to analyse each others' views, to explore the reasons for holding them (both rational and emotional), and engage in analysis of popular media, asking questions about what particular texts aim to do and how they do it. This approach has the advantage that it might allow the exploration of unconscious as well as conscious motivations, the importance of which were discussed in chapter 2. It could be described as being, in some senses 'neutral' — in allowing disagreement to surface and not controlling or censoring pupils — but is certainly not neutral in the sense in which the word is used by Stenhouse.

However, for a teacher to claim neutrality in the sense of not expressing an opinion of her own while not actually being neutral (and it should be noted here that 'neutrality' is not a position possible to achieve), is likely to lead to a belief on the part of the students in the dishonesty rather than the neutrality of the teacher. The assumption of what is, essentially, a dishonest position is questionable on pragmatic as well as moral grounds. Why should students be honest with someone who is lying to them? Assuming an unfelt neutrality is just as liable to lead to students trying to please (or rebel against) the teacher as expressing an opinion.

Secondly, there is no real attempt to define what 'procedural neutrality' means. Does it, for example, mean that teachers will not intervene to encourage silent students to take part in discussions?[11] If some students are silenced (and they are likely to be members of marginalised groups), does not the act of intervention in itself constitute a challenge to taken-for-granted group dynamics in the classroom? On the other hand, if accepted group dynamics are not challenged, is that not a breach of 'neutrality', by allowing powerful groups within a class to continue to dominate?

Thirdly, Stenhouse's characterisation of discussion about 'race relations' as a search for 'truth', without any questioning of what this might mean, is a part of the rationalist tradition of Western thought which is, to say the least, on shaky ground. While there are many mythologies around issues of race (Dickinson, 1982), combating racism is not simply a matter of discrediting them or of gathering the 'truth' (Cohen 1987, 1988, 1989). Reality is experienced in many different ways and one important aspect of education for equality, is that the realities of marginalised groups be validated and explored. However, for this to happen, those in such groups will need to find a voice — which might well be difficult if not impossible with a 'neutral chair'. Moreover, the underlying assumption that racism is simply a matter of prejudice and ignorance (which are, it is implied, never shared by the teacher) is one which ignores the institutional aspects of racism and the processes by which it is produced and reproduced.

Much of Jeffcoate's work (1979, 1984) was part of the Schools Council Project and he continued in very much in the same tradition. Stredder (1978), in her 'illuminative evaluation' of his curriculum development, observes that issues of racism were not usually directly raised by Jeffcoate, though they were dealt with in an open manner when students raised them. This practice is a way of avoiding issues of racism in predominantly white classrooms, where isolated black students may well feel themselves (and be) silenced and where racism is unlikely to be a major concern of the white majority (though racist attitudes and practices are likely to be prevalent).

It may be that black pupils do not wish to enter into discussions of racism when they are in a predominantly white class (one form that silencing of people in oppressed groups takes). So a black child's choice of silence should be respected. It is unacceptable for people from oppressed groups to be compelled to bear the burden of always explaining their experiences to those in a dominant group.[12] A child's need to keep silent, then, should be seen by teachers as a problem for their own teaching rather than as the problem of the child concerned.

Furthermore, although Jeffcoate aims to 'reduce prejudice', his commitment to an ideology of liberal pluralism leads him into the position of affirming the ultimate 'right'[13] of white children (and teachers?) to express their prejudices. He argues that:

> ... [if] in the possession of relevant facts, some children argue that white people are as a group intellectually superior to black people, or come out in favour of repatriation and oppose racially mixed youth clubs or whatever, we have to accept that as their privilege.

(Jeffcoate, 1984, p. 161)

If racial prejudice and discrimination made no difference to the lives and experience of others this view might just about be acceptable. But we know that racism and racial prejudice do damage the life chances and life experiences of black people. It is questionable to assert that members of a powerful group have the right to behave oppressively towards people in a relatively powerless group — and speech can certainly be a form of oppressive behaviour. Furthermore, a commitment to a 'neutral chair' approach in order to avoid authoritarianism does not take into account the democratising of classrooms with which much teaching of controversial issues is concerned (Short and Carrington 1987, p.29).

We saw how the term 'child-centred' has been appropriated by teachers working within a liberal, rationalist and individualistic tradition and selectively interpreted to fit in with this tradition. For the purposes of this book, it is important to note the part which this dominant version of 'child- centred' education[14] has played in giving space to the development of strategies such as those of Stenhouse and Jeffcoate. Too often in 'child-centred' education, the notion of 'starting where the child is' has resulted in 'leaving the child in the same place' with regard to issues of social justice and equality. There are double standards held about this. Yet amazingly, large numbers of infant teachers who feel that they 'can't do anything' about racism because 'children bring it from home', will, without a qualm, impose a total ban on playing with guns in classroom and playground. Evidently the values of the form of liberal humanism adhered to by many teachers makes it comfortable and possible for them to interfere in matters such as fighting and war games but not over racism or sexism. This is not necessarily true of either Stenhouse or Jeffcoate but their insistence on neutrality can lead to positions which do not effectively challenge racism or help children rethink their frameworks for viewing the world (Naidoo 1991, 1992).

Dominant versions of child-centred education emphasise the child as an individual rather than a member of a group, and emphasise learning as an individual process rather than one which takes place within a social context. However, the distinction between the individual and the group is, as argued in Chapter 2 a problematic construction. Individuals live in groups and experience life in terms of their social position. Thus individual girls and boys in this society experience life individually and collectively through their gender, class, racial and sexual identities.

Teachers working within mainstream traditions of child-centred education are more likely to find acceptable those versions of 'racialised' education which view racism as an individual affair. However, such approaches are unlikely to be effective in combating racism in schools. To do this, it is necessary both to pay attention to the complexity of individual experience and subjectivities and to how these are shaped (but not completely determined) by children's social positions and their relationship to dominant and oppositional discourses.

Part of the discourse of 'racialised' education since the early to middle 1980s — and certainly since the Swann Report of 1985 — has been the notion that multicultural or anti-racist education is an issue for predominantly white classrooms and schools as well as for those with high proportions of black students. Arora and Duncan (1985), for example, say that they 'have endeavoured to get away as far as possible from the idea that multicultural education is something for ethnic minorities' (p.2).[15] However, nearly everything written until the publication of Gaine (1987) — including Arora and Duncan's book — dealt almost exclusively with education in schools with large numbers of black pupils. Although there has since been a trickle of books dealing with white areas (Carrington & Short 1989, Hessari & Hill 1989, Epstein & Sealey 1990, Brown et al 1990, Grugeon & Woods 1990, Troyna and Hatcher 1992), the bulk of the literature still concentrates on curriculum content for black children and on dealing with racism where there is a majority or large minority of black pupils.

Furthermore, much suggested curriculum change relies on the use of cultural artefacts (which children can 'experience') and also on having black children in the school and immediate community to act as a kind of 'resource'. Such approaches, well exemplified by Arora and Duncan's collection as well as that edited by Straker-Welds (1984), fall down on three counts. Firstly, they do not provide an adequate way of thinking about or dealing with racism, especially in predominantly (or completely) white schools. Secondly, reliance on artefacts to give children 'first hand' and 'concrete' experience can encourage a superficial approach of looking at the exotic. This approach presents 'culture', as static and as something which ethnic minorities have but the white population does not — except in the form of 'high culture'; certain values the majority white population are assumed to share are seen as 'common-sense' or 'natural' rather than as culturally constructed. This can have the effect of bolstering racism, not combating it. Thirdly, it lends itself to approaches to anti-racist or multicultural education which consist only of a change of curriculum content, instead of approaches that tackle the hidden and overt curriculum, pedagogy and school structures.

The development of anti-racist education

The 1980s saw the development of versions of racialised education which became known as 'anti-racist' rather than 'multicultural'. Brandt (1986) describes the differences between multicultural and anti-racist education in the following terms:

> Anti-racism shares with multiculturalism the obvious assertion concerning the 'multiracial' nature and cultural pluralism of British society. But anti-racism goes further in that it does not see the marginalization, exclusion and devaluation of Black culture by White culture as an error of history but as a product of power relations.

(p.133-4)

One problem associated with the development of anti-racist (and what has become known as 'radical multicultural') education is its frequent reliance on the mere substitution of anti-racist versions of knowledge for racist versions. While this is an important and necessary advance, knowledge about, for example, imperialism and black disadvantage does not in itself automatically lead to the growth of anti-racist perspectives and practices. It is, for example, quite possible to know about how Britain's imperialist adventures ravaged India and Africa, and to believe it to be perfectly justifiable. In South Africa, white people know that black people are exploited, disadvantaged and oppressed, but may justify this by their belief in black inferiority.[16]

Hatcher and Shallice (1983) stress the need for anti-racist education to have 'defined cognitive goals' (p.10), and this is certainly important, but cognition alone is not enough for effective anti-racist education. In chapter 2, we considered the psychic and social investments people have in racism and this highlights the necessity to develop anti-racist education at an affective as well as at a cognitive level.

Social constructionist views of child development and education

'Social constructionist' or 'constructivist' approaches to child development and education, derived from the work of Vygotsky[17] and Bruner, have become increasingly influential. The discourse engendered by this broad approach is important for anti-racist education for a number of reasons: it is based on understandings of how culture and the social context form the basis for learning; it recognises children as actors in the construction of their own realities; and, because of all this, it is possible to develop notions of power relationships in education within the discourse.

Social constructionism in psychology

In contrast to Piaget, Vygotsky saw the infant as a social being. Vygotsky's notion that children construct their understanding and knowledge in a dialogic way with others, including adults, can be understood in terms of 'scaffolding' (Wood et al 1976, Wood 1988) or 'framing'.[18] Bruner (1960, 1968a, 1968b) developed the idea of framing into a notion of the 'spiral curriculum', asserting that anything can be honestly taught at any age. It is not the content of what is taught which matters most , but the way in which teaching is framed. To understand new concepts children need simpler explanations and more scaffolding and, as their understanding increases, they become more and more independent in the handling of those concepts.

More recently writers within the social constructionist tradition have stressed the social and cultural contexts for learning. Thus, for example, where Donaldson (1978) introduced the idea of 'embeddedness' and 'human sense' and Vygotsky (1966) argued that understanding progressed from others to self, Light and Perret-Clermont (1989) have stressed the interactive nature of learning so that 'pragmatic, inter-subjective agreements-in-meaning are seen as lying at the heart of the developmental process' (p. 148). The latter draw attention not only to interaction between experimenter and child, but also to the importance of the wider social and cultural context:

> Socio-cognitive conflict is ... a mechanism which reflects the import-ance of the 'social other' as embodying an alternative perspective to the child's own. Social marking, by contrast, is a mechanism which does not require the physical presence of others, but it is social in the wider and perhaps more fundamental sense that the child's social experience elicited by symbolic means (e.g. the evocation of a norm) provides the framework within which the problem is understood.

> (p. 146)

Even here, the notion that children are active agents in the making of their own knowledge and understandings is not fully explored. Walkerdine (1981) touches on it and Tizard and Hughes (1984) draw attention to children's 'intellectual search' — which they define as the process by which children actively try to understand apparent anomalies in their limited knowledge of the world. This is an idea which allows teachers and others to think about children as active in the construction of their own realities and subjectivities, and therefore potentially active in the deconstruction of dominant ideologies. Urwin (1984), writing within a psychoanalytic framework largely drawn from the work of Lacan, suggests that young children are active in exploring and engaging in power relations. However, she points out that children's exercise of power is shot through with contradictions and that:

> ... taking up relatively powerful positions is not unproblematic. ... It is a moot point whether taking a relatively assertive position within a discourse which itself implies women's subordination is necessarily to the advantage of an individual woman. For instance ... is it advantageous to the little girl to attain power over the little boy through domestic activity?

(p. 317)

I would suggest that it is possible, within the primary classroom, to organise things so that girls are able to assert themselves in contexts which do not imply women's subordination and in which they are invited to deconstruct both sexism and racism. This is discussed in some detail in the next chapter. However, engaging in such reorganisation involves recognising the power relationships involved (including their complexity) and the fact that children themselves construct meanings through their activities in the classroom.

Making meaning through language

Children's construction of meaning is conducted through their use and development of language. Consequently an important feature of the work of Vygotsky, Bruner and other developmental psychologists (for example, Wood 1988) interested in social constructionism, is the stress on language as a means through which children understand and construct their world. This has been taken up and developed further by those interested in language and schooling (Willes 1983, Wells 1986, Edwards and Mercer 1987, Sealey 1990). Sealey (1990), writing about children's knowledge about language, asserts that:

> Children are entitled to opportunities for exploring the phenomenon of language and how it is used, because otherwise 'legitimised and naturalised orders of discourse (are) presented as legitimate and natural' (Fairclough, 1989). In other words, if children are not encouraged to reflect on how language is made to mean what it is being made to mean, they may come to believe that this 'element of their humanly produced and humanly changeable social environment (is) a part of

their natural environment over which they have no control'. One of the first steps in learning how to control language (and thus to increase one's competence via that route) must surely be to develop an awareness that such control is possible.

(p. 48)

If it is true that children construct meaning through language, such ideas about the relationship between language and power and their place in education are clearly an important aspect of the development of anti-racist understandings. This is an area which is under-researched at present, but there are a number of elements of existing research which would contribute to developing it. One example is classroom discourses (Edwards and Mercer 1987) — that is, what teachers and children say and do in classrooms, what assumptions they make, and what they are 'allowed' and expected to say and do in their roles as teachers and children. Another would be the (re)construction of racist ideologies in classrooms and playgrounds (Cohen 1987, 1988, 1989) and also children's construction of notions of justice and 'fairness'. How then would differing frameworks interact and how do children manage to hold both at the same time, in spite of the fact that in many ways they are contradictory and conflicting?[19] And how can the discourse of fairness be utilised in the development of anti-racist education? A third area of exploration would be linguistic and cognitive development, especially concerning meta-linguistic awareness and the possibility of engaging children in the deconstruction of language.

Social constructionism in the sociology of education

The discourse of social constructionism has been taken up and developed by several sociologists of education. This has implications for anti-racist approaches to education. The discourse of social constructionism facilitates dealing with social and controversial issues in the primary classroom. It allows for the development of pedagogies calling for the active engagement of both teacher and taught and for a shift in the relationship between them, since much interpretive sociology reveals that children's experience of school is one of vulnerability, of power relations and of 'trying to protect their dignity' (Pollard 1987, p.4). The making explicit of these understandings and reflection on them is a crucial element of social constructionist approaches to anti-racist pedagogy.

Social constructionism and anti-racism

There is a small body of literature in which social constructionist approaches are used as the basis for anti-racist intervention, including Lee and Lee (1987), Short and Carrington (1987 and 1989), Cohen (1987 and 1989), Epstein and Sealey (1990) and Grugeon and Woods (1990). Much of it takes the form of case studies of classroom intervention and much is situated in predominantly white schools.

All show a commitment to moving towards democratisation of the classroom; commitment to collaborative work within the classroom; rejection of the notion that young children cannot cope with controversy nor with social issues demanding understanding of perspectives other than their own; and a view that 'talking is learning and that talk is not merely teacher-to-child but child- to-child and needs considerable time' (Lee and Lee 1987). Another common theme is that teachers cannot and should not be neutral in relation to racism .

In this chapter we saw how dominant versions of 'child-centred' education in the 1970s and 1980s lent themselves to the avoidance of issues of equality in primary schools and to versions of multicultural education which, since they relied on children's concrete experience, tended to exoticise 'other' cultures through the use of artefacts. Advocates of these versions of racialised education tended to regard racism as an individual problem, to be dealt with on an individual basis. Counter versions of anti-racist education concentrated on the need for teachers to teach a form of 'anti-racist knowledge' in a didactic fashion. Proponents of these views have, in general, focused on the role of the state and society. These divisions have set up false debates. An approach is needed which combines understandings about 'society' with understandings about individual subjectivities. I have proposed that social constructionist interpretations of child development provide a more promising groundwork for developing effective anti-racist pedagogies. Some attempts to do so are described in the following chapters.

References for Chapter 6

1. Donaldson (1978) offers a succinct and accurate summary (pp, 129-146).

2. See Walkerdine (1984) for a full discussion of this approach to pedagogy.

3. By 'concrete experiences', Piaget meant the experience of children in handling objects. For example, they would learn to understand the conservation of volume through frequent experience of pouring liquids from one container to another, differently- shaped one.

4. King (1978), looking up index entries in the Plowden Report, discovered 34 on 'learning' and none on 'teaching'.

5. Compare, for example, Donaldson (1978) with Dunn (1988). See also, Walkerdine (1984 and 1990).

6. See chapter 7 for details of classroom work on the deconstruction of dominant ideologies. See also, Sealey (1990) for discussion of young children's metalinguistic awareness and deconstruction of language.

7. I am indebted to my sister-in-law, Rona Epstein, for supplying this transcript.

8. See, for example, Gray & Satterly 1976 and the reply by Bennett & Entwistle 1976; also Rogers & Barron 1976, McIntyre 1976

9. In using the word 'racialised', I refer to those forms of education where race has been an explicit issue, in contrast to what Kirp (1979) calls 'racially inexplicit' education. I would agree with Troyna and Carrington's (1990) critique of Kirp's view that racial inexplicitness constituted 'doing good by stealth' (pp. 21-22).

10. While this was not the only strategy tried (the others were that of 'committed chair' and drama) I am dealing only with that of 'neutral chair' because of the way it was taken up, particularly by Jeffcoate (1979, 1984).

11. The silencing of people in oppressed groups has been a major theme of feminist writing (for example Spender 1980, Steedman et al 1984) and that of black people and lesbians and gays.

12. Black feminists have written extensively on this subject, both in academic and creative form. See, for example, articles in CCCS 1982 and Donna Kate Rushin's 'The Bridge Poem' in Morgan and Anzaldua (1981).

13. The question of 'rights' is a complicated one, which I do not have space to consider adequately. It is a word used in a number of different contexts from differing points of view, and carries completely different connotations when used in different contexts. It is completely different, for example, to talk of 'a woman's right to choose' and of a man's 'right to father'. It is a word which has been used in an oppositional way, but which, like 'choice' has been successfully appropriated by the Right. This is an issue which has been discussed in various feminist texts. See, for example, Franklin et al (1991).

14. This version is based on Piagetian notions of child development discussed earlier in the chapter.

15. In making this point, I understand Arora and Duncan to mean that multicultural (or anti-racist) education is not something for schools with large numbers of black pupils only. Anti-racist education is for white pupils and staff who affect black experience in schools (whether they be racially mixed or not) and outside schools.

16. It is *possible* that this is beginning to change with recent political upheavals in South Africa, but it has certainly been the case for over a hundred years and continues to be so amongst a large proportion of the white population. Moreover, changes to the

legal institutions of apartheid will not be sufficient to change the relative power positions of black and white people in South Africa.

17. Vygotsky lived and worked in the early part of the 20th century (he died in 1934 at the age of 38) but did not publish much in his lifetime. One book, *Thought and language* (1934), was published shortly after his death. However, his work was little known until the 1960s as it was suppressed in the Soviet Union until the late 1950s and did not appear in English translation until 1962. Later, other pieces by him were collected and translated (Vygotsky, 1978).

18. Vygotsky's own phrase has been rather awkwardly translated from the Russian as the zone of proximal development (ZPD). This is taken to be the area of cognition which children can manage with help and which will be the next (proximal) area of independent understanding which they will develop.

19. This is, of course, also an important question in relation to adults.

CHAPTER SEVEN

WORKING WITH CHILDREN

This chapter consists of case studies of classroom work with children at different stages of primary education and in a number of schools. They demonstrate that, in order to develop effective forms of anti-racist education, it is necessary to work at both cognitive and affective levels, and to 'start where the children are' by working on inequalities with which they are familiar. As children come to understanding their often complex positions in relation to these inequalities, they can come to understand and combat racism.

We can safely assume that all children (even white, middle-class boys) have some experience of oppression. This arises from the ways in which we treat children. Children have very few rights they can exercise freely. Even such apparently basic rights as the right not to be physically or sexually abused, are controlled not by them but by adults.[1] Certainly, all children know how it feels to be told, in peremptory tones and, with little or no consultation or explanation, what to do and how to behave; all children know how it feels to be without freedom of choice, from minor aspects of life (such as whether to eat their greens) to major aspects (such as whether or not they will go to school or, in the case of family breakdown, which parent they should live with). All girls have direct experience of being on the receiving end of gender discrimination, while all boys have had the opportunity to observe this at first-hand.

Note, however, that this does not mean that children are never in positions of relative power, nor that they all experience inequalities in the same way. We considered Walkerdine's (1981) example of boys using their power as males over female teachers in the last chapter, as well as Urwin's (1984) discussion of the way in which girls can exercise power in situations which take for granted the subjugation of women — for example, in domestic play. In the following case studies we see how teachers can organise classrooms so that this does not always happen, and can enable children to reflect on their own experience. Most children have experience of stereotyping others — be it on grounds of age, gender, class, ability, supposed sexuality, ethnic

111

or regional origin — and of being stereotyped. It is these experiences and their unconscious components which must be made explicit and built upon in developing anti-racist education, especially where there are few, or no, black children.

Case Studies

1. Gender, Reading and Race

The work described in this case study took place over the period of a year in Bankhead School. The class was a Year 1 class of 25 children none of whom was black. As the class teacher of a group of five- and six-year olds, I was concerned that all the children should be moving as far as possible towards becoming readers by the end of the year. Over and above this, one of my aims for the year was to introduce concepts of bias and stereotyping to the children, using their reading books and the class library as a resource for anti-racist and anti-sexist learning.

Children clearly do a great deal of work to make sense of the world. The world they need to make sense of is both gendered and racialised and the way they construct meanings, and consequently their identities, is gendered and racialised too (see also chapter 2 for a more general discussion of subjectivity and identity). When children start school they have already come to many understandings about social relations of, for example, gender. Equally children at five have already constructed racialised understandings (see, for example, Jeffcoate 1979, Milner 1983, Lane 1984). A later case study, *A nursery class,* examines the gendered way in which children play and suggests that this can be countered. We are not born gendered or racialised but construct our identities, and we continue to do so throughout our lives. This case study explores some ways in which gender identities and racist constructions can be influenced in the primary school, and how I, as a feminist and anti-racist teacher, tried to challenge dominant ideologies in this regard and to raise some general questions about pedagogy.

Starting points

Teaching in the school was based on thematic, cross-curricular approaches, and I used the various themes undertaken by the class to try to fulfill my aims for the year. As head of Infants, I was able to do things I might not have risked in a more subordinate position.

The themes for the year were 'Ourselves and our families', 'On the move', and 'Books and stories'. Part of the 'Ourselves' theme involved discussion about roles within families. Over a third of the class lived in families headed by a single mother and many fathers were unemployed while mothers worked outside the home. Sharing this information led to discussion about the roles of mothers and fathers in reading books. Almost all the schemes used portrayed stereotypical nuclear family gender roles (for further analysis of popular reading schemes see Lobban 1974, Language and Gender Working Party 1985).

Early in the term, children were asked to respond to a general question about what mothers are like. Their writing tended to follow well worn stereotypes. For example, Alice (aged 5) wrote:

*Mothers[2]

Mothers have to stay at home to look after babies. They do the cooking. My dad helps with the washing up.

However, a month later, after discussion in small groups about what their mothers actually did, Alice (now aged 6) wrote:

*My mum

My mum works on the industrial estate. She gets up early to go to work. My dad gets us ready for school. My mum is tired when she comes home. My dad and me make the tea for her.

Work like this was strikingly in contrast to the children's earlier, more general responses. Alice's writings are typical of the class and of the age group, with their sudden change from the general to the particular.

It is rare for young children to be asked to look again at pieces of writing done earlier in the year. However I felt it was important for them to reflect on the contrast (and also to see how their ability as writers had developed over the month) so I asked the children to spend time comparing their two pieces about mothers. They did so in small groups, each working with an adult (the classroom assistant, a parent or myself). The responsible adult was to ask the children to identify differences between the two pieces of work. Not all groups considered the differences in what they had said. Some confined themselves to a discussion about how neat their writing was, which piece of writing was longer and which one they were more satisfied with. However as a result of contrasting these pieces of work, some children began to wonder where they got their ideas about mothers from — from their own experience or from books and television?

One group of children decided (with guidance) to do a survey of the reading books in the class. They based their survey entirely on the pictures, and produced a block graph showing that mothers were overwhelmingly shown in the kitchen, occasionally doing the shopping and *never* going out to work. On the other hand, fathers were shown going to work (often 'the office') and gardening. A few reading books showed single parent families but even in these, mothers were not shown working outside the home. Anthropomorphised animals instead of people were the main characters used in a number of schemes, but always the animals were portrayed in stereotypical gender roles

The work was displayed and reported to the rest of the class — resulting in a perceptible raising of consciousness amongst the children, especially

113

the girls, of gender bias in their reading books. It became commonplace for children to ask questions like, 'Why don't the books ever show mummies changing the plug? My mum fixed the kettle last night' (question from Becky, age 5, recorded in my diary).

'Girls don't do bricks' — using unpredicted opportunities

An opportunity arose for further work on gender when some of the girls complained that the boys would not let them play with the big bricks. The boys involved refused to give way, insisting that 'girls don't play bricks'. In a round table discussion with the whole class, Clare, Becky and Natasha explained that they wanted to play with the bricks but that the boys wouldn't let them. The boys — Michael, Nathan and Ben — claimed that the girls spoilt their buildings, while the girls said that all the boys wanted to do was build the biggest tower. This led to some indignant interchanges before I asked how they thought the matter could be resolved.

Eventually, at my suggestion, the children agreed that there should be 'girls only' time with the bricks each day. At first only Clare, Becky and Natasha played with the bricks, but the girls' time was gradually extended as more girls joined in. At first the girls were quite tentative in their building, but their confidence gradually developed, and they produced 'buildings' of some complexity, which were much admired by the boys. After three weeks of this we held another class discussion. The girls spoke about how they felt about their experience and most of the boys agreed that girls could make buildings. The class decided that girls and boys should play together, but that 'girls only' times would be re-established should further problems arise. In practice, this became necessary for three further periods of two weeks during the rest of the year.

At this point, I offered children the opportunity to write something about what they thought about the experience. Their written work and behaviour show that some of the boys resented what had happened. Gary (age 5), for example, regularly 'tripped' over the girls' buildings to destroy them and I did eventually deal with him in a disciplinary way by confining him to activities at some distance from the 'brick mat' — even though I generally tried to avoid dealing with conflict in the class through such measures. Brian (age 6) wrote:

> Playing with bricks
>
> I think its no fair to hav girls times. bricks is for boys.

Not all children (or adults) are ready to take on new understandings! Nevertheless, there is also evidence that some boys began to reconsider their positions. For example, Michael (age 6) wrote:

*Playing with bricks

I used to think girls don't do bricks. Then we made a girls time for bricks. They made really good houses, specially Clare. Now I like to play with Clare in the bricks. We make lots of good buildings.

Later in the year some of the children discussed with me why the boys had these notions about the girls' abilities with bricks, and why many of the girls shared these notions. The children started by agreeing that girls and boys could all use bricks. Then the conversation turned on why the boys had reacted as they did. One boy expressed puzzlement, but then said that perhaps it was because the girls had never played in the bricks in his play group, and 'mostly you don't see pictures with girls in the bricks'. One of the girls expressed the view that it was not fair, and that boys always had more fun 'because you're allowed to play football and everything'.[3] Some of the girls' complaints about the ways in which boys dominated and interrupted them, took up more space in the classroom and 'never listened', though expressed in the language of six year olds, bore a striking resemblance to consciousness-raising discussions experienced in the Women's Liberation Movement.

I describe these events at some length because I believe that they illustrate the difference, in both teaching style and outcome, from anti-sexist and anti-racist education approaches which introduce positive images and concentrate on heroines rather than heroes but do not allow children to reflect on their own experience, still less to pick up possibilities for development from the activities of the children themselves. My strategy differed also from individualistic approaches, which treat conflict as a problem of individual behaviour.

It was essential that the children related their work to their direct experience of stereotyping others and fulfilling stereotypical roles themselves. It was also important that the issue was not seen in terms of some boys being 'naughty' but that the children themselves explored the social dynamic involved. Thus, when the girls complained about how their play with the bricks was restricted, I seized on the opportunity to discuss with the children their own perceptions of gender roles in their play, to help them reflect on their feelings and understanding about them and to change not only their behaviour but also their understandings. Obviously, the situation with the bricks arose more or less by chance, but situations offering similar possibilities to develop work around gender and/or race occur in all classrooms, provided the teacher is willing to hear what the children are saying and flexible enough to respond to them appropriately. However this does take time, and time may well be increasingly difficult to find as the National Curriculum and testing are fully implemented.

Challenging racism — making opportunities

During the second term, the theme 'On the move' took the class out of the school, into the neighbourhood and the town centre. Here they noticed black people in the shops — the local corner shop was run by a Pakistani family — and in the town centre. An important event for the children was a visit by Grace Hallworth, a black writer and story-teller who impressed the children enormously. They showed her their books and stories, and described what they had found about women in reading books. She asked the children if any of their reading books had pictures of people who looked like her. This led to an immediate search through the reading books:

> We looked at all our reading books in our class we found some pictures of people who looked like Grace. Mostly the people in the books looked like us. Also Ramu and Sita [characters in the reading scheme *One, two three and away* by Shelagh McCullough] dont look like us and they dont look lik Grace. Some of our libry books have pictures of people like Grace though.

(John, Lucy, Gail and Michael)

During the third term theme on 'Books and stories', the children were introduced to the idea of reviewing books. We discussed, and I produced, a sheet on which they would write book 'reviews' for a file in the class library. Children had the option of either writing about the stories under particular headings, some pertaining to representations of gender and race (such as what black people or women were doing in the story and whether this seemed accurate or 'fair') or of ticking pictures of 'happy', 'sad' and 'neutral' faces to indicate their enjoyment of story and pictures and whether the stories showed women and black people doing interesting things.

By the time the children started to do these 'reviews' they were already accustomed to expressing their opinions and feelings verbally, both generally and specifically in relation to books. The writing of 'reviews' for use by other children both validated their opinions and feelings and gave them a reason for writing, since they could see it was useful and purposeful for others. The questions on the review sheets helped them to express their opinions and focus their attention on particular aspects of their reading.These questions had evolved from work the children had already done during the course of the year-long concentration on books and stories.

Learning from people other than the teacher

Parents were constantly in the classroom reading with, talking to and helping the children. These parents were involved in the discussions about bias in books and most of them accepted the validity of the approach. I also felt it necessary to include the parents who could not or chose not to come in to the classroom. Accordingly, I made a point of discussing issues concerning the teaching of reading and the exploration of bias with every parent in the

116

class, either after school or at parents' evenings. Some parents were concerned about the approach, particularly about the introduction of questions about race into the reviews and at least one couple were actively hostile. But even they could see that their children were learning to read and enjoying the activity. In discussions with parents, I invited them to contribute their own short reviews of books their children brought home and added these to the class collection.

Parents had been involved in the development of their children's work throughout the year and the writing of reviews gave them a particular role. This was an important part of creating an understanding among parents of what I was trying to do and in gaining their consent to what, at the beginning of the year, had seemed a strange and unfamiliar approach. The vast majority of parents are concerned that their children should be happy at school and that they should make progress in the 'basics'. Involving parents in the learning process helped them understand what was involved in the approach and drew them into working with their children, so that they were able to see clearly the gains their children made in learning the 'basics'.

The theme on 'Books and stories' was extended to a collaborative project with a Year 6 class (aged 10-11). Each of the older children was to write a book intended specifically for one of the younger children. Consequently, the older children spent a considerable time visiting my classroom, reading favourite stories with 'their' child and discussing with them their interests and preferences. The stories were then written, illustrated and bound by the Year 6 children and presented to 'their children' at a joint 'party' to which the Schools' Libraries staff were invited. This project led to considerable discussion about the processes by which books appear. Children looked at dedications, wrote to favourite authors asking them about why and how they had written certain books (and had several replies). Children began to understand the concept of books being written from a particular point of view and for a specific audience. For example, Mark (age 6), wrote:

> My best book is *Rosie's Walk.* Pat Hutchins rote it for a little child. Pat
> Hutchins liks farms She goes on holiday in the cuntry.
> (May 1986)

They also began to understand that not all books written are actually published, that there are people who decide which books should be published, and that these decisions are subjective. In particular, they noticed that there were considerably fewer books by black authors and about black characters than there were by white authors and about white characters. Some of the children questioned this, particularly after Grace Hallworth's visits. Even at their age, many of the children showed an astonishing sophistication in their understanding, which developed considerably over the year. Their own reactions to books were validated, and they discovered that they did not have to enjoy every book they read and that they were allowed to say that a book was boring or unfair. Although they did not use words like 'stereotyping' or 'bias' (though introduced to such terms), they did have a basic understanding of these concepts —which they expressed in terms of 'fairness' — and which they could build on in the future.

Questions raised by the case study

This case study illustrates the culture of one classroom, and also the possibilities open for a primary school teacher (who has the same pupils for a full year) to plan long-term objectives, as well as dealing with the day to day and week by week planning which is the stuff of most teaching. It is characterised by a willingness to take risks — to 'go with' the children's interests, using them to highlight and develop some of the issues crucial in developing education for equality. Had the dispute over the bricks not arisen, it could not have been taken further, into study and reflection on gender relations. On the other hand, it would have been very easy to settle the incident when it arose by simply insisting that the boys share with the girls and telling them not to be 'silly'.

Would these children have been able to think about issues of race in the same way without having had the experience of first exploring some issues around gender which arose from their own experience? Some people concerned with developing anti-racist education argue that starting with other forms of inequality or oppression is, at best, diversionary and, at worst, a strategy for (racist) white teachers to avoid dealing with racism. While this can certainly be true at times, I believe that starting with areas of oppression which are meaningful for children actually enables them to acquire far deeper understandings of racism. The fact that they have thought explicitly about their own feelings in relation to inequalities of which they have direct experience is more effective in terms of countering racism than either instructing them about 'other cultures' or telling them that black people are badly treated and that it is wrong to be racist.

2. Poetry and dance

Starting points

The work described in this section took place at Badminton Middle School with two Year 6 classes. There were two black children (one of African-Caribbean and one of Pakistani origin) in one class and one child of Indian origin in the other. The class teachers were the deputy head, Dave, (who, we saw, in chapter 5, to be the main force behind involving the Project in the school) and Erica, a probationary teacher. The differences between these two classes are interesting, since Dave's greater confidence and understanding meant that he felt able to follow up our collaborative work when I was not there, whereas Erica confined the work to the half-day per week of one half-term when I was present.

I had also worked with the two classes the previous term for one day each week introducing teachers and children to creative movement, which was totally new to the school. As a result the other teachers in the school asked for some in-service training on dance. Though I would have prefered to work directly with the teachers after school, they were not willing to so I agreed to work with these two classes, other members of staff being released from teaching at different times to observe lessons.

Creative movement is one of the areas of the curriculum about which many teachers feel insecure, and it is also one which has been completely left out of the National Curriculum (except as part of PE). This is, of course, to be expected from a curriculum which is almost entirely concentrated on the cognitive, since dance is pre-eminently to do with the expression and understanding of feelings. Dance is one of the most stereotyped activities taking place in school. More even than cooking or woodwork, it is constructed as gendered and frequently offered only to girls — particularly where dance takes place only in voluntary clubs.[4] Dance has a bad name among both teachers and children — partly due to the ubiquitous *Music and movement* BBC programmes, which (probably because of the very nature of broadcast as fixed and pre-recorded) have not allowed for children to develop their own movement through using their own imaginations and bodies.

The aim of this part of the project was to undermine the stereotypes of dance as a girls' activity, to challenge the children's imaginations, to see how far working through dance would enable them to understand the meaning of poems and — since the poems chosen were partly about the experience of racism by black poets — to increase their understanding of the meaning of racism in real situations. Poetry, too, is a medium which engages with the unconscious and is therefore particularly suitable as a vehicle for deconstructing unconscious investments in racism and sexism (see chapter 2).

The National Curriculum Orders on English (DES and the Welsh Office 1989a) have, as one of their Attainment Targets at Level 3, to:

> demonstrate in talking about stories and poems, that they are beginning to use inference, deduction and previous reading experience to find and appreciate meanings beyond the literal.

> (AT2, Knowledge, skills and understanding in reading, p. 8)

However, nowhere in the English Orders relating to the primary phase is there any Statement of Attainment about writing poetry, although the Cox Report (NCC 1988b) included it in the Programmes of Study 8 to 11. Nor do any of the National Curriculum documents suggest how children might learn 'to find and appreciate meanings beyond the literal'. Along with the rest of the National Curriculum, the emphasis in English is very much on cognitive aspects of learning, and the Orders move further than the Cox Report from recognition of the affective aspects as being important.

119

Developing the work

In deciding what stimuli to use for the creation of dance with the children, I chose a poem for each class by a black author — 'Dreaming Black Boy' (in a slightly cut version) by James Berry and 'Still I rise' (again slightly cut) by Maya Angelou. We began with the children exploring shapes and movements to express words and phrases that I had provided. Next, the children examined the texts in groups, deciding which words could be used as the basis for movement.

These words were used as the basis for developing sequences of movement for each verse. Each group then chose one verse to work on more intensively. In Dave's class, children followed up the movement lessons in my absence, discussing the meaning of the verse, writing about their own experiences and emotions triggered by the poetry and writing poems around these experiences and emotions — of wanting more attention from parents and teachers, of the frustrations of not being in control of their own lives, and of wishing to be able to remain strong in the face of their own pain. One girl wrote:

> When I read the poem [by James Berry] it makes me think of all the times when I've wished for more attention. Sometimes in class discussions I sit there wishing I could say something. I often know what I want to say but think that the others might think I'm stupid I'm scared that they might laugh at me. At home I often feel as if my parents don't take much notice of me and I wish I could tell them.

(Beverley, age 11)

Another child wrote the following poem:

Wishing
I wish my mum
Would know that I was there.
Wish she didn't look at me
With a worried frown.

I wish my dad
Was home when I came in.
Wish he had time

To take me to football.
I wish my teacher
Didn't always ask the others.
Wish he could see
That I was trying too.

(Glenn, age 11)

120

Erica did not work in the same way and, though we did discuss the poem in the course of the movement lessons, the children did not develop the same level of understanding as those who were given the opportunity for more discussion and exploration. There is no writing from this class to indicate their level of involvement with or understanding of Maya Angelou's poem.

There was no specific discussion during the development of the dance about the fact that the authors of the poems were black — though the children had seen pictures of them both and the class working on 'Still I rise' were shown a video of Maya Angelou performing it. Towards the end of the half-term, when the dance was ready for 'performance' to other children in the school, I took an afternoon with each class to discuss their poem with them and to allow them to evaluate the work they had done with me over two terms.

The children in Dave's class were clear in their opinion of Berry's poem. They discussed both its universality, relating it to their own experience and the work of other children, and pointing out that it was partly about being black. All the children said that they had experienced some of the feelings expressed in the poem. One of the white boys said that he thought that teachers often took less notice of black children and of quiet children. A white girl observed that it was not only teachers who did this, saying 'I've noticed how, in the playground, the black children are often on their own, or they go round together, even when they are not in the same class'. Ian, the African-Caribbean boy, who was highly articulate, spoke of his feelings about being one of only two black children in the class but added, 'It's not so bad now. The others in this class don't make fun of me so much. I find it easier to tell them when I'm feeling hurt or upset and mostly they take notice of that'.

The children in Erica's class understood that 'Still I Rise' was, in part, about the history of black Americans — one of them commented that 'It's about them being slaves and about racism, innit?' However, very few of them spontaneously related the poem to their own experience . When I drew their attention to Maya Angelou's statement at the beginning of her performance that the poem was for 'everyone who goes to bed feeling terrible, gets up in the morning, meets someone who says "How're you", grins and replies "Hi, I'm fine, and you?", children responded that they could relate to that feeling, but had not got it directly from the poem.

Evaluations

The children's evaluations of the work they did in Dave's class concentrated on the affective domain. They all agreed with the group which identified the most important thing they had learnt to be: 'We discovered that we learn better in groups'. Other contributions to the evaluation included statements such as, 'We learnt to listen better', and 'We're more careful what we say, because we don't like to hurt each other's feelings'. Their main complaint was that they had spent too long polishing the dance, they did not like working barefoot 'because the hall floor has splinters and is dirty' and some of the girls said that they did not enjoy working in groups with boys.

The other class, which had spent less time in detailed response to their poem, were less positive in their evaluations. Although they had enjoyed the work, they definitely regarded it as 'special' — an extra added on to the usual curriculum and not to be taken seriously in the same way as subjects like mathematics and science. They failed to make the same connections with their own experience that the other class had, and there was less evidence of change in their understandings of racism. The one black girl in the class would not contribute to the class discussion, though she did make some contribution in her small group.

Questions raised by the case study

This case study raises questions about the isolation of work around issues of equality from other parts of the curriculum, and about the effectiveness of work of this nature when the teacher herself is not confident of the pedagogy involved. The purpose of developmental work must be that teachers learn to adopt new ways of working — but, as we saw in chapter 5, change involves risk, so must offer perceived rewards. For a teacher struggling with her probationary year, in a school where formal didacticism was valued and rewarded by the head the risks were too great.

That anti-racist education should 'permeate' the curriculum has been widely asserted. While this case study confirms this, it also raises the question of how such permeation is possible when the teacher is (or feels) unready. Is it better to provide the kind of 'extra' I was able to do, or to support the teacher in other ways until she feels ready to handle issues of racism confidently herself?

Also important is the silence of the single black child in Erica's class. In the last chapter we noted how black children in predominantly white classes might not wish to make themselves vulnerable by discussing their experience of racism with white teachers and children, and this identified a problem which teachers need to address without putting black children 'on the spot'.This was precisely such a case.

3. A nursery class

Starting points

The work for this case study and the next took place in Jennings School.[5] Of the handful of black pupils, there were none in the reception class and two in the nursery class. I worked in each of these classes for one day a week. In both classes the teachers were concerned about the relationships between the boys and the girls, and all the staff were concerned about playground behaviour. The whole school adopted the theme 'People at play' for the term, and the staff as a whole drew up a flow chart in collaboration with teacher advisers. The nursery teacher, Naomi, was also eager to develop a closer relationship with the parents of children in her class and to involve them more in the children's learning.

The first Cox Report (NCC 1988b) was published in the middle of that term, and Naomi and I decided that we should incorporate some consideration of the suggested requirements for Attainment Target 1 (AT1), Speaking and Listening, into our work. As the Cox Report points out:

> In a child's development listening precedes talking; talking precedes literacy. Each feeds the other and is in turn developed. Children are highly motivated from the earliest stages to respond to the world around them and to communicate their needs; they have expectations, experience pleasure and enjoy success.

(para. 2.2)

Cox states further that, 'before arrival at school, fortunate children will have listened ... to a rich variety of talk and been encouraged to express themselves to sympathetic adults' (para 2.3).[6] We decided to monitor the variety of talk in which the children engaged in the light of suggested levels of attainment in AT1. Although the children in the class were much younger than seven, when they would be assessed for Key Stage 1 (KS1), the acquisition of language is a continuous process which, for children with unimpaired hearing, begins at birth and continues throughout childhood (perhaps throughout life). In taking account of this continuity of development, we concentrated on AT1 as appropriate at this phase of schooling, even though a few children in the class showed signs of emergent writing and several were aware that print carries meaning.

Work in the nursery began with a period of observation by Naomi and me, helped by the use of a video camera which, despite poor quality of sound, gave us a good chance to examine in detail the relationships between children and between children and the adults in the classroom. What was revealed was a pattern of play which was almost exclusively single sex: certain toys (cars, bricks, railway) used almost exclusively by the boys, but both boys and girls playing in the play house and with the dolls (though seldom together).

Outdoor play, too, was divided by gender with the boys gaining almost exclusive control of the 'bikes' (i.e. various wheeled toys). Here, however, the girls made positive efforts to use these outdoor toys, but failed because the boys were always first to get them, whereas they made little or no effort to play with the 'boys' toys' inside. The children's interactions with adults, both inside and out, were almost exclusively in terms of organisation of the class (e.g. requests for permission to play with certain toys), discipline and some directed teaching.

Making opportunities — changing patterns of play

Accordingly, our first move was organisational in terms of the outside toys — girls and boys were to alternate and a list kept of which children had actually had a chance to play on the 'bikes'. We also arranged that one of the adults would regularly play with the children using one or other of the indoor 'boys' toys' and that there would be some periods for girls only to play with these toys. This began to change the girls' relationship to these toys and also gave adults the chance to talk with the children while they were playing. We also organised times for only girls to play with the cars.

The video revealed an intriguing difference in the way the girls and boys tended to play with the cars. Whereas the boys would run them round 'roads', have 'crashes' and 'stop for petrol', the girls were much more interested in looking at them carefully, turning them over, opening and shutting the doors, examining the wheels, and only began to use them on the 'roads' after much careful consideration. It seemed as if the girls were much more tentative, possibly because they had less experience of playing with them. As the girls became more familiar with the cars, they started to develop imaginative play with them but even this was gendered. While the boys continued to use the cars as described above, the girls tended to elaborate a complicated story line — which, in one game, involved taking children to school, doing the shopping, going to work and rushing back to pick up children at the end of the day.

Children were invited, in small groups, to watch the video themselves, so that they could comment on their own play. The first showing, as might be expected, was taken up with children trying to spot themselves on screen. At a second showing, children were asked particularly to notice with whom they played and, in one particular sequence, to discuss the fact that there was a group of boys playing with the train set while a girl sat around the edges, obviously trying to join in but being prevented from doing so. Although comments were not sophisticated, and the children were unable to discuss their behaviour in the manner of the slightly older children described in the case study *Gender, reading and race,* one boy did offer the comment that 'Dorothy looks sad' and another boy who had been in the group playing with the cars, said 'Next time I'll ask her to play with me'.

Looking at images

Through this work it quickly became clear that these three and four year olds were able to reflect on their own play and relationships, though not at a very sophisticated level. They were certainly able to recognise and discuss their own and other children's feelings in particular situations, as was further demonstrated by later work with them using the photopack *Behind the scenes* (DEC 1986). This pack, intended mainly for use in INSET, consists of photographs of children and adults in schools engaged in a variety of activities. Children discussed which photographs they particularly liked and why.

The DEC photographs are of black as well as white children, and this gave the children the opportunity for discussion about issues of race. Alex, for example, said he didn't like the pictures of 'blackies'. Alex lived with his white mother but his father was black. He became quite distressed by the suggestion that he himself might be called 'blackie', denying that he fitted this description. Later, one of his friends, trying to comfort him, said 'We do like blackies. I'm your friend', while another commented 'if you're nice, it's OK'.

While it might be argued that the children were working within a racist framework which excludes known black people from expressed prejudice, it does seem to me that, within the limits of their own experience, they were seeking a formula which would be comforting to Alex and which had the potential for challenging racism. This seemed further confirmed when one of the children involved in the original discussion came up to me some time afterwards and said, confidentially, 'There's nice blackies and nasty blackies, ain't there? Just like us'.

Using stories

Listening and responding to stories is an important source of learning for young children, both in terms of the acquisition of language and literacy and in 'explor[ing] realms of fantasy and reality' (NCC 1988, para 2.9). As Wells (1986) says:

> ... stories have a role in education that goes far beyond their contribution to the acquisition of literacy. Constructing stories in the mind — or *storying*, as it has been called — is one of the most fundamental means of making meaning; as such, it is an activity that pervades all aspects of learning.
>
> (p. 194, original emphasis)

It is therefore unsurprising that the use of stories forms such an important part of teaching and learning in nursery and primary classrooms. Furthermore, self-narration is a key feature of the construction of subjective identities — we tell ourselves and others stories which help us learn 'who' we are. As a way of making and understanding meaning, stories and storying form an essential part of education for equality in nursery and primary education.7

Also as part of the project that term we used the story *The tiger who came to tea* (Kerr 1968), a favourite, as it is in many nursery and infant classes. The story is about a little girl, Sophie, who is at home with her mother, when there is a knock on the door. It turns out to be a very large and hungry tiger. The tiger eats everything in the house, from sandwiches to tins in the cupboard, and drinks everything in the fridge and all the water in the tap. After he leaves, Sophie cannot have a bath, because there is no water left and her mother is worried because there is nothing at all for tea. But when

125

Sophie's father arrives home he solves the problem, taking Sophie and her mother to a cafe. The next day Sophie and her mother go shopping, buying, among other things, a very large tin of tiger food.

The book was read to the children as a class and again in groups which then dramatised it in a variety of different ways: with Sophie at home with her father; without a father at all; with Sophie and her mother solving the problem for themselves; and so on. In one version, Sophie and her mother went to an Indian take-away. Figures for use on a felt-board were placed in the classroom for two weeks, and the story was played and replayed in many different forms, allowing the children to talk about their own experience of family life. They observed that they did not eat only sandwiches and baked beans, but also food from a variety of places and traditions.

We set up an interest table, with foods from different countries and packaging with labels in a variety of languages, to alert the children to the existence of languages other than English in the community. There was more work in groups on themes arising from the story, which the children chose themselves in discussion with an adult. One group painted pictures of tigers in the zoo and in the jungle. Another made up a complicated story to explain how the tiger came to be wandering around the streets — according to them he had escaped from a zoo, because he was unhappy in a cage. A third group made a collage of pictures of food Sophie might have given the tiger.

The children in this particular class were able to manipulate story telling, through dramatic role-play, and achieved all the Statements of Attainment for Level 1 of Attainment Target 1 (Speaking and listening)[8] in the English Orders (DES and Welsh Office 1989) and achieved four out of five items at Level 2 — excluding only 'respond appropriately to a range of more complex instructions given by a teacher, and give simple instructions' — although they were only three and four years old. That is, they were able to:

participate as speakers and listeners;

describe an event, real or imagined;

listen attentively to stories and poems, and talk about them;

talk with the teacher, listen and ask and answer questions.

(DES and the Welsh Office 1989, p. 3)

Notwithstanding Kenneth Clarke's concern when he was Secretary of State for Education, about the need for drilling and practice, it was clear that the children did not achieve these levels through rote learning or decontextualised exercises, but through their enjoyment of a story and their satisfaction in having the power to organise themselves and retell the story in ways of their own devising. Furthermore, in telling their different versions of the story, they were able to begin to explore gender roles and to consider some different styles of living than that depicted in the original book.

Evaluation by the class teacher

In evaluating this work Naomi commented that, in terms of her own perceptions:

> the project has taught me to be more open minded. To see situations in different ways, to introduce them to the children in different ways, to question their purpose. To let the class express themselves more, rather than being spoon fed. By making the children decide for themselves something is for example wrong, right, fair, unfair, by evaluating the situation. To make the children more *responsible*. By presenting facts and letting children make their own judgements, you can introduce the issues of racism, sexism etc.

Some questions arising from the case study

Some of the questions relate to the teaching of language — particularly speaking and listening. The fact that these very young children were able to deal so competently with targets supposed, by the Secretary of State and the National Curriculum Council to be suitable for children two or three years older may indicate that the National Curriculum targets are wrongly defined in terms of age. However I think that it has more to do with the engagement of children in the work. The question is not 'What can children do at particular ages?' — which constructs them as developing through discrete age, maturity and/or intelligence related sequences — but, instead, 'How can we support children's learning so that they can best develop and use language and complicated concepts?' And when we explore answers to this question, we should keep in mind the findings of social constructionist psychologists and sociologists concerning the use of 'scaffolding' in teaching and learning, discussed in the previous chapter.

The notions of 'ages and stages' relate to Piagetian and Plowdenesque ideas about teaching and learning, which have so influenced the pedagogic discourses of primary classrooms. It is a matter of some concern that the way in which the National Curriculum is tied to key stages to be assessed at particular ages (seven, eleven, fourteen and sixteen) may tend to strengthen rather than weaken the attachment of teachers to such ideas which, in the field of developmental psychology, have been largely discredited. The second Cox Report acknowledges 'the problems in defining a linear sequence of language development' (DES and the Welsh Office 1989, para. 14.5). However it remains to be seen how teachers will respond to the demand that 'language development must be conceived, fostered and assessed in terms which are broad enough to accommodate variations between individuals' (*ibid*, para. 14.5). They might end up adopting the sequential nature of the National Curriculum, adhering to the suggested ages for various levels of attainments, and eschewing the flexibility suggested in the Cox Reports.

127

Another question arises out of Alex's distress over the discussion about 'blackies' — a word which he had himself introduced. Obviously, when children are distressed in this way it is important to give them support and comfort. But what is the best way of doing so? Should it be through cuddles and physical comfort? Should the child's denial that he was black have been glossed over? When his white friends offered comfort — by saying, effectively, 'We love you, even though you are black', should our response, as teachers, have been to welcome their attempts or to try to raise with them the implications of what they were saying — bearing in mind how young they were? My own response was to give Alex plenty of cuddles, to allow the children to respond spontaneously, but also to try to shift the discussion away from Alex's own situation to the idea that we cannot judge people until we know them — but I am still not sure that I chose the best combination. One might argue that it was foolish to allow the issue of race to be raised by using pictures with black children in them, but should we not recognise an important aspect of children's identities and lives, not make any opportunities available to shift young children's existing perceptions and prejudices?

4. A reception class (Year R)

Starting points

This class was also in Jennings School and I spent as much time there as in the nursery. Much of the teaching was concentrated on developing co-operative learning and much time devoted to co-operative games. Children were, again, very gendered in their play, the girls tending to choose creative activities such as painting and drawing and play in the 'house' while the boys tended to concentrate on puzzles and construction toys. The playground was a major issue for these children, many of whom found playtimes a frightening and unfriendly experience. This came out very strongly in discussions with children from the Year 6 class when they came into the classroom to observe the younger children at play and to work and play with them. The older children were working on suggestions to improve playtimes and they discussed this with the reception children, who wanted more teachers and more games to play.

Developing the work

There was also considerable work on the topic of friends — who they were, what made someone a friend and why they liked certain people. Children drew pictures of and wrote about their particular friend:

*I like Petra because she lets me share her toys.
(Jacqueline, age 4)

*John is kind to me. He has curly hair and brown eyes.
(Ian, age 5)

They came to the conclusion, after much discussion, that 'it doesn't matter what your friend looks like, so long as they're kind and share things' (Lorna, age 5, in a class discussion).

Children also looked at the photo-pack, *Behind the scenes* (DEC 1986) described above. One photograph in particular, of a crying girl of South Asian origin, led to a discussion of name-calling in which the children started to talk about how they felt when they were called names. A subsequent brain-storming exercise on name-calling drew out words such as 'sad', 'cross' and 'upset'. After this, the one black child (of South Asian origin) spoke about how she felt when she was called 'Paki', saying it 'makes me want to run away'. Two of the boys, who, in discussion of the photographs, expressed dislike of black people ('But not Tara'), were challenged by other children, and one little girl asked them, 'How can you not like people you don't know'?

The class teacher and I did not play a 'neutral' role in this interchange, but took part in the discussion, backing up the children who were challenging the prejudiced comments and trying to get the boys to reflect on the reasons for their feelings. While this discussion did not succeed in actually changing the attitudes of the boys involved, it was important both because of the support offered to the black child in the class and because it meant that the children involved in the discussion were enabled to explore their feelings more deeply than if such comments had been simply contradicted, or the boys 'told off'.

Later work revolved around feelings, with the children discussing in small groups and writing about what made them feel happy and sad. One little girl wrote:

*I am happy when my friend asks me to play. I am sad when we fight.

(Samantha)

while Tara (the girl of Pakistani origin) dictated the following:

*I hate being called Paki. Paki means horrible and I'm not nasty. Playtimes is bad, but it makes me better when Sally plays with me and tells them nasty ones to go away and stop being rude.

(age 5)

This work, around the theme 'People at play', started to uncover some of the racist incidents that were regularly happening in the playground. The teacher had been unaware of them since they took place out of earshot of the adult on playground duty. It was not only the children in Year R who indulged in racist name-calling, but their class teacher and I felt that it was important to deal with it in the classroom situation. Our dilemma was that we did not wish to put Tara through a constant reiteration of her experiences. We were pleased that she had trusted us enough to dictate the passage quoted above and to talk to us, but we did not want to make her the centre of the class discussion. We therefore decided to return to the general question of name-calling.

We read out to the whole class a number of passages in which the author expressed distress over name-calling, and asked the children how they felt about what we had read. A number said that they were reminded of how unhappy name-calling made them, so we then asked them how they thought it could be stopped and how it should be dealt with by the teachers. The children came up with a number of ground rules like 'think of something nice to say to everyone in the class each day' and 'tell a grown-up if someone makes you unhappy'. Their strongest wishes were to be allowed to choose whether or not they went out to play and for there to be more teachers in the playground — both, unfortunately, measures impossible to implement in a school with hard-pressed and overworked teachers. One possibility, which was being discussed by staff as we left the school, was to have a group of fourth year Juniors coming into the Infant playground each day to take care of some of the more vulnerable younger children.

Questions arising from the case study

The most intractable question arising from this case study is how we balance the interests of teachers and children when they are in conflict — as they were in terms of playtimes. Teachers need a break during the day, but children need to be spared feeling intimidated and miserable in the playground. Perhaps the idea of having the older children take care of the younger ones was implemented and did work — this was not something I found out on return visits to the school.

Another question is how best to help young children consider complex political and social issues like racism in ways that they understand. I believe that this case study, together with the previous one and the one based in Bankhead School, illustrates how very young children (under the age of 7) can engage with difficult issues and reflect on their own feelings and reactions, provided they are given appropriate opportunities, encouragement and scaffolding to do so. This willingness to engage in reflection and empathy are the basis of any attempts to change children's (and adults') feelings of racial prejudice. However, the freedom to do so depends heavily on a classroom culture which is democratic and open. And such a culture will not be arrived at unless considerable thought and attention are given to structures and practices within the school and classroom and without going through a lengthy and possibly painful process of change.

5. What happens when there are more black children?

Starting points

The last school I worked in during the course of the project was Dover School. The Year 6 class (aged 11) was doing a project on 'Change', suggested by the children themselves because they wanted to think about their impending transfer to secondary school. Work started with a brainstorming session, during which the children identified the following main themes:

economic changes — wages and prices;

education — progression through the system and the ERA;

personal changes — opinions and attitudes, belief, thought, emotion;

demographic changes — migration, racism, population growth, birth control;

technological change

the changing position of women;

the ecology and the environment.

They then sorted out their ideas into four categories:

Things that have changed.

Things that need changing.

Things that change by their very nature.

Things that we'd like not to change.

This provided the framework for the term's work.

Looking at images

The children started by making 'time lines' of their own lives, noting the changes they considered important. At the same time they mapped their names on to a wall map of the world, showing places with which they had connections — a process which revealed connections, for both black children and white, with many different parts of the world. The children brought in photographs of themselves as babies or young children, and we took photographs of them during the second week of term. They used these pictures to illustrate their time lines and to reflect on the ways in which they felt they had changed physically, intellectually and emotionally.

Work using photography is particularly useful in enabling children to explore ideas about images and stereotyping (Cohen 1987 and 1989, Davies

1989). In discussing their own photographs, the children explored issues of how they liked to be seen and how they felt they actually appeared in their photographs. They worked on captioning photographs in a variety of situations, with groups swapping photographs so that each group worked with the photos of children in another group. In addition all the children made up captions for their own and each others' photographs. They were astonished, and sometimes indignant, at the variety of captions produced. This led to discussion of newspaper photography and captioning followed by producing alternative captions to newspaper photographs of their own choice so that the meaning of the photograph was changed. This work proved to be a particularly useful preparation for looking at advertisements later in the term.

Later the children used a photopack, *Working now* (DEC 1989), designed for work on gender roles. This was extremely successful, the children finding much of interest to discuss in the photographs. At one point, when the children had been working with photocopies of half a photograph and were subsequently given the originals, there were gasps of, 'God, it's a woman!' This led to vigorous discussion of the stereotyping of women and men and of racial stereotyping. One of the black boys in the class was able to speak of his frustration at being expected to be good at football, 'when really I'm quite average'.

Discussion about stereotyping led on to work on advertisements though unfortunately there was no time to look seriously at television advertisements and the combination of image and language that goes to make up their impact. However children did devise some of their own advertisements and talked about the hidden messages of advertising which they categorised as: those which 'make you think you'll be sexy'; those which 'make you think everyone else has got one'; and those which 'make you think you'll have a happy family'. We could profitably have done considerably more with the children on making and deconstructing advertisements[9] but were constrained by time so could not develop this aspect of the work as fully as I would have liked.

Learning from people other than teachers

In the next stage of the project, children interviewed each other about their lives as a preparation for interviewing older members of their families. They needed considerable practice in interviewing. At first they tended to ask questions which required one word answers — usually 'yes' or 'no' —such as 'Do you like this school?' with no follow-up 'Why?'. Interviews were taped and discussed in class so that children could work out what kind of questions and follow-up questions would elicit longer and more revealing answers. The interviews with older members of their family, which they carefully prepared in groups in the classroom, revealed a wealth of life experience covering migration, bereavement, falling in love, marriage and divorce. Children discovered differences and similarities between the lives of their parents and grandparents and were particularly interested in the ways in which tastes, in for example music, had changed. They were also fascinated by revelations about conflicts between their parents and grandparents.

Discussions were held with groups of children about their interviews, and two discussions were taped. What follows is part of the transcripts:

1.   With the class teacher, Clive Jenkins (CJ), and 5 children — 1 African-Caribbean boy (Ian), 2 Sikh boys (Kuldeep & Gurdial), 1 white girl of Scottish origin (Rachel) and one white English girl whose family came from the West Midlands (Anne):

Anne: Well, my gran, she said ... when she was grown up she said it was easy to get jobs round here...

Ian: (interrupting) Right. My grandad came here because of the jobs. He came from Jamaica to work on the buses. I've still got family in Jamaica — like I put on our map — and I went to visit them when I was small. It was really good there.

CJ: What about the rest of you? Have your families always lived in Birmingham, like Anne's, or have they moved, like Ian's?

Rachel: My mum and dad came from Scotland. It wasn't so long ago. I can still remember it ... we came when I was little.

CJ: Did you start school there or here? I can't remember whether you were in our infants or not?

Rachel: No ...when I was a middle infant.

CJ: Were you happy about it?

Rachel: Well, umm, not at first, 'cos everyone else had friends already and it took ages to make friends. But then it was good.

Kuldeep: My dad came first and she [his mother] was left behind in India. He came and lived with my brother-cousins[10] and my uncle and aunty. My mum said that she had to wait a long time to come. ... Like, my brother, he was two when my dad went away and he was ten when we came. She was, she was...

Gurdial: (interrupting) Yeah, me too. That's almost like my family. My dad came first and then my mum. But they wasn't married when he came. He came back to India to get married and then they came here together.

CJ: Did they have any problems with coming?

Kuldeep: Well, my mum, she said it was really horrible. Because she had to wait so long, and then it took ages, when there was enough money, it took ages to get a .. umm, a, what's it called?

CJ: A visa?

Kuldeep: I think so (unintelligible) lots of questions — like when she got married and if my dad was really her husband and that ....

Anne: But that's not fair! She wouldn't say he was her husband if he wasn't.

CJ: Why do you think the immigration officer asked her those questions?

Kuldeep: Something, something to do with the law.

CJ: Do you know anything about the law, about immigration laws?

Kuldeep: Well, my dad says it's something about not wanting so many Indian people here. He says it's because of racism.

Rachel: Yes, but, when there's lots of people, English people, without jobs, you can understand ...

Anne: But you're not English either. You said your mum and dad and you, you came from Scotland.

CJ: Perhaps we should try to find out more about the immigration laws. I think Ms Epstein has got some books, or maybe we could get something from the library.

Note that the word and the concept of 'racism' were introduced by one of the Sikh boys. 'Racism' and 'sexism' were part of the vocabulary of these children before I started working at the school and, in this class, the black children felt safe to raise the issue of racism and did so several times during the course of the work. This was something that happened very rarely in classes I worked in with few black pupils. In classes which were all or virtually all white, questions of racism seldom arose spontaneously and the problem for the teachers was how to raise the subject without becoming didactic and over-prescriptive.

In this case it was the teacher, Clive, who asked whether the immigrant parents had any problems. He and I had previously discussed the possibility that the black children in the class might have had personal experience of discrimination by immigration officials. It was also Clive who brought this part of the conversation to an end when it seemed to be provoking conflict, by suggesting that the children might find out about immigration legislation — though he did leave open the possibility of further development of the subject. When we listened to the tape afterwards and I pointed this out to him, Clive said that he had been totally unaware that he had done this. It seems likely that if the discussion had not been deflected by the teacher, the racism expressed by one child might have been effectively challenged by other children. But teachers are trained to try to avoid conflict — to the extent that we supress opportunities for enabling constructive engagement of ideas between children. Of course, it is not only in areas of controversy that we direct children's discussion and contributions, sometimes completely unconsciously (Edwards and Mercer 1987). However, in teaching for equality particularly, it is vital to make explicit those agendas and ground rules which usually remain implicit and hidden.

The child who challenged Rachel's statement —basically rehearsing the myth that black people come to England to take jobs which rightfully belong to the 'English' — was Anne, the other white girl.[11] She homed in on the fact that Rachel herself was not English but did not directly challenge her underlying belief. Sadly, an opportunity was missed to develop the children's ideas and understandings about one of the most prevalent mythologies about black immigration — that 'they came here to take our jobs'. Indeed, by moving away from this discussion, the challenge to Rachel was in incomplete and personal, and the idea of fairness — introduced earlier in the conversation — not raised. Yet in a school and classroom where the majority of children are black and where racism and sexism are constantly under review it was not surprising that Rachel's statement would be challenged, and it was good that it came from another white child. However, I think there are very real concerns about the outcome of the discussion.

The other discussion followed a somewhat different course:

2.   With myself (DE) and 4 children — 1 Turkish boy (Amir), 1 girl of Kenyan Asian origin (Nira), 1 Black Country boy (John) and 1 Irish girl (Cath),

Nira: My dad, he was about 13 when he came from Kenya. He told me how he didn't want to go really, but my grandad said they had to and, and like they had lots of money, but they couldn't bring it all, but my grandad was still happy to come here, because people, Asian people was having a really bad time and then, afterwards, after his family was here, then other Asians, they found it harder to come here.

DE: Did you ask your grandparents about this?

Nira: No. My grandad died a few years ago and my grandma, she don't speak a lot of English so I didn't interview her.

DE: What language does she speak?

Nira: Panjabi

DE: Could you interview her in Panjabi? I think that would be really interesting.

Nira: My Panjabi .... I don't speak it very good.

135

DE: That's a shame. You know, my grandmother didn't speak much English, and I can't manage any Yiddish, and I've always been sad that I didn't get to know her very well because of that.

Amir: My mum don't speak good English. At home we speak Turkish.

DE: Does anyone else speak a language which isn't English at home?

Nira: Sometimes my mum and dad speak Panjabi, when they don't want us to understand

Everyone laughs.

DE: Yes, my parents used to do that with Yiddish. It's really annoying isn't it?

Nira: Yeah .... but I do understand a bit.

DE: What about you two, you haven't said anything yet?

John: Well, we only speak English ..... my mum and dad send us out when they want to talk private.

Cath: Us too.

DE: Have either of your parents migrated, like Nira's and Amir's?

Cath: My family comes from Ireland. I go to Irish dancing lessons.

John: We always lived round here. My granny and grandpa live in Sandwell and my other nan lives up the road from us.

DE: Those of you whose families have moved, did you find out why they moved? I mean, Nira spoke about how Kenyan Asians had to leave, some of them quite quickly and without being able to take all their money and possessions with them. That was, they left because of what was happening in the country they came from.

Amir: My mum and dad, they came because they didn't have no money in Turkey.

Cath: Yeah, mine too. They said Ireland's much poorer. There ain't no jobs for people there.

DE: All my grandparents left Russia because they were Jewish, and there was a lot of anti-semitism there — Jews were very badly treated.

Cath: That's like racism, isn't it?

DE: Yes.

Conversation then turned to discussion of the children's conflicts with their parents, mainly around irritations about household chores. The subject of racism had come up mainly as a result of my own intervention but the children did not follow it up. There was, however, discussion about language — the loss of a language over three generations and about parents finding ways to keep things secret from their children, often through the use of language. The issue of language and bilingualism is an important one for anti-racism. It is an area about which strong feelings are aroused — and one which the government has been particularly anxious to play down.

Following these and other group discussions, the children worked in groups to write up their collective findings from their interviews. Each of the five groups tackled a different subject:

1) changes in musical fashion and popularity;

2) problems to do with migration and immigration;

3) conflict with parents now and then;

4) rules by which children were and are brought up; and

5) experiences at school.

Ideally I would have liked one group to have considered changing language use for both bilingual and monolingual families but only two children who expressed interest in working on this aspect of the interviews. Both were of South Asian origin and, although offered the opportunity to work as a pair, they decided rather to work with some of the other children, and finally both worked on experiences at school.

The written work of the group dealing with migration and immigration is most relevant to the present book. It explored, at some length, people's reasons for moving. In this class, the children were aware of both push and pull factors — the availability of employment, the hope of a better life, the cost of housing and, in Nira's case, quoted above, government action. Several children in the class had parents who had come to Britain separately; the experience of Gurdial's mother was not unique. The children worked hard at understanding the provisions of British immigration law which I summarised for them as simply as I could. They did not find this easy but were carried through the complexity partly by anger at the experiences of their own parents and some of their classmates'. Here is part of what they finally wrote about it:

> We found it hard to understand about Immigration Laws. We thought that the laws seemed unfair, if they meant that people like G's mum could be asked whether they were really married. We think they make the laws hard to understand on purpose because it doesn't say people from India and Kenya can't come here, but we know from our interviews that they do find it hard to get in.

137

Group projects

During the second half term, the children worked in groups on 'Campaigners for change'. They were given free choice of subject and library time in which to make the choice. Two groups selected Martin Luther King; other figures were Rosa Parks, John F. Kennedy, Guru Nanak, founder of Sikhism; and Jane Addams (of whom I knew nothing), an American feminist, abolitionist, and social reformer, founder of Hull House[12] in Chicago. The children were allowed to present their work to the class in any way they felt appropriate and chose a range of methods of presentation, from dramatisation to lecture. For their information they depended mainly on published material available in the school and local library, though the Sikh boys brought much information into the class about Guru Nanak.

Two groups found difficulty with their work. All that the Rosa Parks group could find about her was that she refused to move to the back of the bus in Montgomery, Alabama and so started the bus boycott. Eventually they dramatised this incident in their presentation. The group doing Kennedy found a wealth of material, but almost nothing about changes he had made. They finally decided, in the end, that Kennedy 'didn't really get much done. If he hadn't died probably no-one would be very bothered with him' and presented their findings as a litany of books they had looked at and people they had asked, which confirmed that he made little change in American society. Finding much more written about his foreign policy, they concluded that what he had actually done was to do with the Bay of Pigs, the Cuba crisis and American involvement in Vietnam.

One of the groups investigating Martin Luther King concentrated on developing their ideas about how black Americans felt when he first started appearing on national television. In order to help them with this I started them off by helping them read Alice Walker's essays, 'Choice: a tribute to Martin Luther King' (1973) and 'The civil rights movement: what good was it?' (1967). In the latter essay she writes:

> What good was the Civil Rights Movement? If it had just given this country Dr King, a leader of conscience, for once in our lifetime, it would have been enough.

> (p. 128)

The children took this theme and Alice Walker's writing to develop a short play with two scenes. The first scene was about the impact on a black child of first hearing Martin Luther King speak on television, and the second showed the same girl, some years later, marching on Washington DC. The other group studying King gave a history of his life and ended with a reading of part of his famous speech 'I have a dream ...'

The group researching Jane Addams gave a dramatised version of her visit to Britain and the founding of Hull House, while the group investigating Guru Nanak concentrated on explaining the basic tenets of Sikhism.

The playground again

Another major part of the work was focused on the playground — at the changes made since the children had started at the school and at what more might be done. An important factor in the children's commitment to their work was the head's undertaking that he would discuss with them any recommendations made about the playground and, jointly, try to formulate ways of making changes to meet their needs. During the course of this work, one group spoke to children from some of the other classes. The topics discussed ranged from the fairness or otherwise of teachers and dinner supervisors to name-calling and racist abuse. Although present at the interviews, I took a minimal part, leaving the children to act as interviewers. Here Chris and Diana are asking the questions, but both also take part in the general discussion:

Chris: Do you think the dinner ladies are always fair when there's been fights?

Alan: I do.

Diana: Sometimes, I think the children aren't very fair to the dinner ladies. I think they're a bit cheeky. I was once.

...

Bob: I think the dinner ladies are fair, but sometimes they don't let you get a word in edgeways to try an explain why it happened and how it happened.

Alan: Yeah, they try and like, say themselves, what's happened.

DE: What about teachers at playtime?

Alan: I think the teachers are fair enough at playtime

Bob: I think they're fair, but I don't think they give you time to explain why you did it. There's always going to be a reason why you've done something.

Diana: And, if it's your teacher that you're in their class, umm, it sometimes carries on into the lesson as well, so you waste another lesson as well.

...

Diana: Do you think it's fair that sometimes the teachers just listen to the oldest people?

Alan & Bob: No.

Bob: I don't think they do anyway.

139

| Alan: | No, I don't think they do either. I think they give both, every-body who's involved a chance to actually speak. |
| Diana: | But I think, that when they listen to part of the story they say, well this is what I think and the children know that that's not what's happened. |

.....

| Diana: | Do you often hear name-calling? |

...

Chris:	There is some racism.
Bob:	Yes, there is still some racism.
DE:	Can you give some examples?
Bob:	Like, umm, paki ...
Diana:	I haven't heard much in the school, but I have heard lots on the street and that.
Bob:	You don't really hear a lot of racism in the school.
Chris:	People who are in the school, you know when they're not in lesson time, they can, kind of, be racist. People who come to this school, when it's not actually school time.
Diana:	Have you ever been a victim of name-calling?
All the others:	Yes!
Bob:	I used to be called four-eyes a lot, and four-eyed monster and everything ....
Chris:	I used to be called chocolate eclair. I didn't like that.
DE:	How does it make you feel, being called names?
Bob:	Angry, but, normally, if you've got really good friends, they'll come and comfort you..
Chris:	That's if you've got any friends.
Diana:	It makes you angry inside. It makes you, umm, feel as if you want to hit them or call them a name back. Sometimes it makes you retaliate.
Bob:	But if you do, you know that you'll get in trouble yourself.
Chris:	So it's best to ignore them, or go and tell a teacher. That's what we're always being told.

140

This discussion reveals the range and depth of the children's thinking and understanding about their interactions with each other and with adults. The subject of racism came up quite spontaneously among these children. The fact that racism should be a topic of conversation introduced by the children on several occasions in this school reveals a clear difference from the other schools I worked in which had very few black pupils.

Evaluations

At the end of the term children were given an evaluation sheet to fill in anonymously. It included the following questions:

1.   What do you feel you have learnt during this topic?

2.   What have you enjoyed about the topic? Why?

3.   What parts of the topic have you found less interesting, or not enjoyed? Why?

4.   What do you think about the ways of working we have used?

Replies to question 1 ranged from those which stressed the affective dimension such as:

I have learnt to discuss and express feelings with people;

I have learned to discuss and share my ideas with others;

I have learnt to share problems;

to the more factual, such as:

I have learnt about some of the people who have tried to change;

I have learnt something about Martin Luther King;

I have learnt more about Jane Addams;

and included such statements as:

I feel I've learnt more about equal rights for blacks;

I have learnt that boys and girls should be equal and black and white people should be equal.

Answers to question 2 included the following:

acting and finding out about [Jane Addams] was good fun;

you learn about a person and you can talk in your groups;

working together because if I got stuck then my friends helped me;

you get a chance to express your feelings about the world and its problems;

141

the interview with my parents because it gave me an opportunity to compare my life to my parents;

I enjoyed learning about Rosa Parks because it was fun I was never bored and it made me realise racism is worse than I thought;

Doing research because it's exciting. You don't know what you're going to find out next!

I enjoyed working in a group because we could share our ideas with each other.

On the question 'What parts of the topic have you found less interesting, or not enjoyed? Why?' eight children replied that they had found it all interesting. Others said they did not enjoy the writing because 'there was so much to do' and 'someone else always had the book'. For one child, the worst bit was:

writing it up in best because you already know what you're going to write and its very slow. Sometimes it gives me cramp when I write a lot.

A couple of children complained of too much talking, one said that 'I didn't really learn anything from [brainstorming]' and another that:

I found interviews with parents [boring] because most of my answers were yes or no and I couldn't build on it.

Another child found doing the life history intrusive 'because we had to reveal information that we might not have wanted to'. There were also several who found that doing the advertisements 'wasn't very lively'.

The class teacher's evaluation of our joint work with the class and its effect on him was that he was:

more open now. More confident to give opinion. More aware of personal feelings of minority groups. [I] used to have a fear of raising racist issues in case that was perceived as 'being racist' — frightened of opening a 'can of worms'.

He now felt more:

ready to listen to children's points of view and to incorporate them into the planning stages. Children have done more collaborative work than I would have planned. The groups have changed more frequently. Questioning has been more open- ended.

His reservations were that:

Group work and discussion has created a problem with generating individual work for assessment. I still feel I need to be prescriptive with formal written expression as far as presentation and quantity [are concerned].

Questions arising from the case study

This was a particularly rich case study poossibly because it took place on such favourable ground. Children were well-versed in taking responsibility for their own work and working collaboratively so were able to achieve a good deal in a short time. Clive was more than willing to pursue the theme of 'Change' when I was not in school and to extend it to cover all areas of the curriculum. Thus there was considerable continuity and every time I went into the classroom there were children bursting to tell me what they had done during the week since my last visit. This enthusiasm — on the part of the teacher and, consequently, the children — was another important factor.

Returning to the way Clive effectively stopped the children's discussion about racism, how much does it matter if such an opportunity is missed? We cannot possibly be fully aware at all times of opportunities presented — and it seems to me that this is not a matter for guilt and self-flagellation, but for reflection and consideration, so that teachers can become more aware of what is happening when it is happening rather than when it is too late.

We also have to clarify the role of the teacher when a racist statement either goes unchallenged by other children, or is taken up and built upon — or when, as in this case, the challenge is itself problematic. For reasons explored in the previous chapter teachers cannot afford to be neutral — but there is a fine line between, on the one hand, enabling children to challenge racist and sexist statements and behaviour and challenging them oneself in a constructive way and on the other, driving such feelings underground so that they become part of the school counter-culture.

Finally a question arises from my conversation with the children about their interviews: what one does when trying to develop anti-racist education if the children do not take up the opportunities to discuss racism. What should be the balance between pushing our own agenda and keeping agenda-setting within the power of the children? I perceive a fine line between enabling children to make use of opportunities to reflect on their own constructions of the world and forcing them to do so, so that they begin to resist the teacher's efforts. There are constant judgements to be made in any classroom. How they are made must depend on conditions in that particular class and other contingent factors such as time available for discussion.

If we are to open up opportunities for ways of reducing classroom prejudice, we need to find approaches like that described in the case study, which allow children to explore their feelings and retrieve and use relevant information, while at the same time enabling them to challenge one another's prejudice. But we have to take care not to become intrusive. It is likely that in future we will increasingly encounter problems related to assessment of individual children. I think it vital that we raise this question in connection with assessment and the National Curriculum.

Conclusion — towards an anti-racist pedagogy

'Child-centredness': mainstream or anti-racist?

The approaches described in these case studies can be said to be in some cases 'child-centred'. However, they differ from dominant versions of child-centred education in some important ways. Firstly, they reject the notion that children cannot decentre just because they are young. The pedagogy is built upon social constructionist ideas about child development and learning and on the assumption that how much children can do depends as much upon the scaffolding provided — by the teacher and other children — and upon previous experience, as on the notional 'ability' or 'maturity' of individual children.

Secondly, children and schools are regarded as part of society rather than as in some way removed from it. Children, then are not 'innocent' of the common-sense ideologies and teachers are not expected to be neutral or to allow sexist, racist or homophobic language and behaviour go unchallenged. What is important is *how* the challenge is made. It is far more effective if it comes from the children's peers and if they can begin to deconstruct their own prejudices. However, as Cohen (1989) says:

> The shift into a different frame, where the teacher no longer acts as an interlocutor but actively takes sides, is a necessary moment in most anti-racist work; as long as it is explicitly signalled and the children are aware that the rules of the game have changed, there should be no problem. But how the teacher now confronts the issues is crucial.

> (p. 53)

Very often the role of the teacher will be to recap selectively and amplify what other children have said, so as to highlight alternative ways of looking at the world and to strengthen the voices of the children providing such alternatives by means of what Cohen calls a 'positive echo'.

The culture of the children or the culture of the school?

Most writing about 'multicultural' or 'anti-racist' education focuses on the culture of the children and of ethnic minority groups; often recording a litany of black disadvantage. This is the most obvious difference between the canon and this present work. My case studies emphasise the cultures of the classroom and the building of trust amongst the children and between them and the teacher, to allow issues to do with racism to be raised in ways which help children to challenge racist ideas and common-sense. This, it seems, is the best way towards *Changing Classroom Cultures*.

Much of the debate around multicultural and anti-racist education has been about 'cultures'. Justified complaints about ethnocentrism in the curriculum have generated provision of artefacts, books about 'other' cultures, and other 'multicultural' resources, nourishing the process, the idea that only black children have a 'culture' or are 'multicultural'. One head teacher, for example, at the end of an INSET session told us about the 'one multicultural child in my school — and she's so middle class that we don't notice'! This may be an extreme instance of the 'multicultural' equals 'black' (and working class) idea. But it is not an uncommon notion, and it carries with it assumptions about the supposed cultures of black people — that they are static and unchanging, without any organic relationship to the society within which they exist.

In practice, of course, all of us live within and in relationship to a variety of 'cultures', which change and which we ourselves alter through our activities. Moreover, teachers who make assumptions about the 'home culture' of children in their classes on the basis of their names, religion, colour or place of origin are almost certain to get it wrong. Children in Birmingham, white or black, are, for example, equally likely to eat 'Indian' food or fish and chips. Religious observance changes over time and from family to family. Language too changes, and English and minority languages are influenced by each other.[13] We can see this particularly clearly in American English, which employs numerous words, phrases and constructions from many different languages. Any teacher considering her or his own family's history and culture would find that much has changed over time, just as the children in case study 6 did, when they interviewed their parents and grandparents.

The case studies in this book are characterised by a classroom culture which not only allows but actively encourages questioning, expressing feelings and opinions and respecting the feelings and opinions of others. Thus, for example, in case study 1 on *Gender, reading and race,* we saw that the girls felt able to complain about their exclusion from playing in the bricks, while the boys were able to listen to and heed what they were saying. Equally, the other case studies were conducted in classrooms where, for the most part, children were able to articulate their feelings about a range of experiences, including, for the black children, racism.

Planning for both cognitive and affective learning

The case studies share one characteristic: both cognitive and affective learning are planned for. I would argue that all learning has both a cognitive and an affective dimension — learning multiplication tables for example, can evoke either pleasure or pain but is not, and cannot be, a neutral experience. Whether teachers plan for it or not, their pupils will experience their learning as either positive or negative. Traditionally, educationists talk of the cognitive and affective domains, implying that these are discrete areas of experience and learning. In fact the cognitive and affective are integrated. This book argues that all cognitive learning will involve an affective dimension. On the other hand, as shown particularly clearly in case study 2 (*Poetry and dance*), learning which involves a high level of emotional involvement and exploration of feelings enables children (and adults) to make cognitive gains.

However, while provision for both cognitive and affective learning are a necessary condition for developing anti-racist education, their presence alone is not sufficient to ensure that the education offered children will be anti-racist, anti-sexist or anti-heterosexist in effect. In order for this to happen, one must also plan for — and take advantage of opportunities offered for — explicit exploration with children of issues of inequality.

Exploring issues of equality.

In all the case studies, discussion of and learning about equality issues, particularly race and gender, were consciously included both at the planning stage and when opportunities were presented by the children's interests as the work unfolded (see, for example, the incident with the bricks in the first case study) were used. Unless this is built in, children might never question racial or gender inequalities, simply because they are never asked to think about them, in which case, even the most 'caring' school can discover that racial bullying has been going on unsuspected and unchallenged over a long period — as happened when Tara spoke about being called 'Paki' in the reception class. An essential part of an anti-racist pedagogy, then, is to create, as well as take, opportunities to explore equality issues with children, in a context in which they feel they are safe and can express feelings, while making cognitive gains.

Although none of these case studies was unproblematic, they provide pointers for good practice in the area of anti-racist education. Attention has been drawn to the ways in which both national politics and micro-politics shape the possibilities for and the forms of anti-racist developments. I have stressed that children are active in the construction of their own identities and in making their own meanings from the experience of social relations. In so doing, they construct and reconstruct dominant ideologies and discourses, but are also able— given the scaffolding in the form of counter-discourses— to deconstruct them and develop new, anti-oppressive meanings. The very complexity of identity and the contradictory nature of our positions within various discourses means that possibilities are always present for opposition — even within the context of a piece of legislation as seemingly all-embracing as the ERA. It is these possibilities which must be developed through micro-political interactions in schools and classrooms if anti-racist education is to survive and effective forms of education for equality be developed.

References for Chapter 7

1. Kelly *et al* (1991) point out that the current strategy of teaching children to say 'no' is ineffective. In their survey, 90% of those unable to stop the abuse used the same strategies — of physical resistance, saying 'no' and avoiding the abuser — as those who escaped or avoided the assault. Furthermore, the supposedly 'imaginative' Children Act 1990 insists that social workers and others engaged in 'child protection' must work in partnership with 'parents', who often include the person (usually the father) who has perpetrated the abuse.

2. All examples of children's writing which were dictated to an adult are marked with an *. In other examples original spellings and punctuation have been maintained.

3. This was at a time when some of the women staff were in dispute with the Head over whether girls should be allowed in the football team!

4. However, in recent years there have been attempts to break down this view and work done at Harehills Middle School in inner-city Leeds has led directly to the establishment of such well-known all-male troupes as Phoenix. The growth of male interest in dance is not unproblematic, since it is an area of female excellence which could be 'taken over' by men to the detriment of women dancers.

5. This work is drawn on in Epstein and Sealey (1990).

6. It should be noted, here, that all hearing children , not just 'fortunate' ones, live in an environment which abounds with different kinds of talk.

7. This should not be taken to imply that they do not form an important part of later phases of education. However, this book is concerned with the education of primary phase children.

8. Level 1 Statements of Attainment are:
   a) participate as speakers and listeners in group activities, including imaginative play.
   b) listen attentively, and respond, to stories and poem.
   c) respond appropriately to simple instructions given by a teacher.
   (DES and Welsh Office 1989, p. 3).

9. See Sealey (1990) for a description of more extensive work with children on advertising.

10. In Panjabi the same word is used to signify brother and male cousin, and similarly for sister and female cousin. Thus it is common for children whose first language is Panjabi to use the formulation 'brother-cousin' to signify a male cousin.

11. My experience, that it is very often girls who do challenge such statements, is confirmed by Naidoo's research (1991, 1992).

12. Hull House was one of the first 'social settlements' in north America. These settlements acted as neighbourhood social welfare agencies. They were distinguished by the fact that members of staff lived and worked in the neighbourhood. The social settlement movement began in 1884 with the founding of Toynbee Hall in London.

13. See Rampton (1989) for an account of this process at work in school.

References for Chapter

BIBLIOGRAPHY

AHRENS, G., FAROOQUI, A. and PATEL, A. (1988) Irrespective of race, sex, sexuality ... in CANT, B. and HEMMINGS, S. (eds) (1988), *Radical Records. Thirty Years of Lesbian and Gay History,* London, Routledge.

AITKIN, M., BENNETT, S.N. and HESKETH, J. (1981) Teaching styles and pupil progress: a re-analysis, *British Journal of Educational Psychology,* 51, pp. 170-86.

ALEXANDER, R.J. (1984) *Primary Teaching,* London, Holt, Rinehart and Winston.

ALTARF (1984) Challenging Racism, London, ALTARF.

ALTARF Primary Workshop (1981) *Race in the Classroom. Teaching Against Racism in the Primary School,* London, ALTARF.

ANDERSON, B. (1989) Education and anti-racism: strategies for the 1990s, *Multicultural Teaching,* 7,3, pp. 5-8.

ANDERSON, D. (1982) *Detecting Bad Schools. A Guide for Normal Parents,* London, Social Affairs Unit.

ANGELOU, M. (1986) Still I rise in ANGELOU, M. And Still I Rise, London, Virago.

ARNOT, M. (1981) Culture and political economy: dual perspectives on the sociology of women's education, Educational Analysis, 3, 1, pp. 97-116.

ARNOT, M. (1986) *Race, Gender and Education Policy-Making, (Course module for Open University course E333, Policy Making in Education),* Milton Keynes, Open University Press.

ARORA, R. K. and DUNCAN, C. G. (eds) (1986) *Multicultural Education. Towards Good Practice,* London, Routledge and Kegan Paul.

AULD, R. (1976) *William Tyndale Junior and Infants School Public Inquiry: A Report to the Inner London Education Authority,* London, ILEA.

BALL, S. J. (1987) *The Micro-Politics of the School. Towards a theory of school organization,* London, Methuen (republished by Routledge).

BALL, S. J. (1990a) *Markets, Morality and Equality in Education,* Hillcole Group Paper 5, London, Tufnell Press.

BALL, S. J. (1990b) *Politics and Policy Making in Education. Explorations in policy sociology,* London, Routledge.

BALL, S.J. and BOWE, R (1991) Micropolitics of Radical Change. Budgets, Management, and Control in British Schools in BLASE, J. (ed) *The Politics of Life in Schools. Power Conflict and Cooperation,* London, Sage.

BALL, W. and SOLOMOS, J. (1990) Racial equality and local politics in BALL, W. and SOLOMOS, J. (eds) *(1990) Race and Local Politics,* London, Macmillan.

149

BARKER, M. (1981) *The New Racism. Conservatism and the Ideology of the Tribe*, London, Junction Books.

BEN-TOVIM, G., GABRIEL, J., LAW, I. and STREDDER, K. (1986) *The Local Politics of Race*, Basingstoke, Macmillan.

BENNETT, S.N. (1976) *Teaching Styles and Pupil Progress*, London, Open Books.

BENNETT, S.N. and ENTWISTLE, N. (1976) Rite and wrong: a reply to A chapter of errors, *Educational Research*, 19, 3, pp. 217-235.

BERKSHIRE LEA (1983a) *Education for Racial Equality: General Policy Paper*, Berkshire Education Authority.

BERKSHIRE LEA (1983b) *Education for Equality: Summary Leaflet*, Berkshire Education Authority.

BERRY, J. (1988) Dreaming black boy in BERRY, J. *When I Dance*, London, Hamish Hamilton.

BHABHA, H. (1983) The Other question, *Screen*, 24.

BHABHA, H. (1986) Of mimicry and man: the ambivalence of colonial discourse in DONALD, J. and HALL, S. (eds) *Politics and Ideology*, Milton Keynes, Open University Press.

BIKO, S. (1978) *I Write What I Like*, London, Heinemann,

BOURDILLON, H. (1991) Whats Happening in History?, *The English and Media Magazine*, 25, pp. 16-18.

BOWLBY, J. (1951) *Maternal Care and Mental Health, Report to World Health Organisation*, New York, Shocken Books.

BRANDT, G. (1986) *The Realization of Anti-Racist Teaching*, Lewes, Falmer Press.

BROWN, C., BARNFIELD, J. and STONE, M. (1990) *Spanner in the Works. Education for Racial Equality and Social Justice in White Schools*, Stoke-on-Trent, Trentham Books.

BRUCE, T. (1987) *Early Childhood Education*, London, Hodder & Stoughton.

BRUNER, J. S. (1960) *The Process of Education*, Cambridge, Massachusets, Harvard University Press.

BRUNER, J. S. (1968a) *Processes in Cognitive Growth: Infancy*, Worcester, Massechusetts, Clark University Press.

BRUNER, J. S. (1968b) *Towards a Theory of Instruction*, New York, W.W. Norton & Company by arrangement with Harvard University Press.

BRUNER, J. S. (1972) Nature and uses of immaturity, in WOODHEAD, M., CARR, R. and LIGHT, P. (eds) (1991) *Child Development in Social Context 1. Becoming a Person*, London, Routledge in association with the Open University (first published in *American Psychologist* 27, 8).

BRUNER, J. S. (1982) The organization of action and the nature of adult-infant transaction in VON CRANACH, M. and HARRE, R. (eds) (1982), *The Analysis of Action*, Cambridge, Cambridge University Press.

BURGESS, H. and CARTER, B. (1992) Testing, regulation and control: shifting education narratives, paper given at CEDAR International Conference, Warwick University.

BURGESS, H. and CARTER, B. (forthcoming) Bring out the best in people: teacher training and the real teacher, British Journal of Sociology of Education.

BUTLER, J. (1990) *Gender Trouble. Feminism and the Subversion of Identity,* London, Routledge.

CARBY, H. (1982) White woman listen! Black feminism and the boundaries of sister-hood in Centre for Contemporary Cultural Studies. *The Empire Strikes Back,* London, Hutchinson.

CARRINGTON, B. and SHORT, G. (1989) *Race and the Primary School. Theory into Practice,* Windsor, NFER-Nelson.

CARRINGTON, B. and TROYNA, B. (1988) Children and controversial issues in CARRINGTON, B. and TROYNA, B. (eds) *Children and Controversial Issues: Strategies for the Early and Middle Years of Schooling,* London, Falmer.

CENTRE FOR CONTEMPORARY CULTURAL STUDIES (1981) *Unpopular Education,* London, Hutchinson.

CENTRE FOR CONTEMPORARY CULTURAL STUDIES (1982) *The Empire Strikes Back,* London, Hutchinson.

CENTRAL ADVISORY COUNCIL FOR EDUCATION, (1967) *Children and Their Primary Schools,* (The Plowden Report) London, HMSO.

CLARKE-STEWART, K.A. (1988) The effects of infant day care reconsidered: risks for parents, children and researchers, Early Childhood Research Quarterly, 3, pp 293-318.

COARD, B. (1971) *How the West Indian child is made Educationally Sub-Normal in the British School System, London,* New Beacon Books.

COHEN, P. (1987) Reducing Prejudice in Classroom and Community. Report on the first year (mimeograph), PSEC/CME Cultural Studies Project, University of London Institute of Education.

COHEN, P. (1988) The perversions of inheritance: studies in the making of multi-racist Britain in COHEN, P. and BAINS, H. (eds) *Multi-Racist Britain,* London, Macmillan Educational.

COHEN, P. (1989) Tackling Common-Sense Racism, (mimeograph) Cultural Studies Project, Annual Report 1988/9, University of London Institute of Education.

COMMITTEE OF INQUIRY INTO THE EDUCATION OF CHILDREN FROM ETH-NIC MINORITY GROUPS (1981) *West Indian Children in our schools* (the Rampton Report), London, DES/HMSO

COMMITTEE OF INQUIRY INTO THE EDUCATION OF CHILDREN FROM ETH-NIC MINORITY GROUPS (1985) *Education for All (the Swann Report),* London, DES/HMSO

COMMITTEE OF INQUIRY INTO THE TEACHING OF MATHEMATICS IN SCHOOLS (1982) *Mathematics Counts (the Cockcroft Report),* London, HMSO

COOPER, D (1989) Positive images in Haringey: a struggle for identity in JONES, C. and MAHONY, P. (eds) *Learning our Lines. Sexuality and social control in education,* London, Women's Press

COX, C.B. and BOYSON, R. (eds) (1977) *Black Paper 1977,* London, Temple Smith.

COX, C.B. and DYSON, A.E. (eds) (1969) *Fight for Education: A Black Paper,* London, The Critical Quarterly Society.

COMMISSION FOR RACIAL EQUALITY (1986) *Teaching English as a Second Language: Report of a Formal Investigation,* London, CRE.

COMMISSION FOR RACIAL EQUALITY (1988a) *Learning in Terror,* London, CRE.

COMMISSION FOR RACIAL EQUALITY (1988b) *Living in Terror,* London, CRE.

COMMISSION FOR RACIAL EQUALITY (1988c) *Medical School Admissions: Report of a formal investigation into St. Georges Hospital Medical School,* London, CRE.

COMMISSION FOR RACIAL EQUALITY, (1985) *Swann, a Response from the Commission for Racial Equality,* London, CRE.

CULTURAL STUDIES, BIRMINGHAM (1991) *Education Limited: Schooling, Training and the New Right Since 1979,* London, Unwin Hyman.

DALE, R. (1989) *The State and Education Policy,* Milton Keynes, Open University Press.

DAVIES, A. (1991) Piaget, teachers and education: into the 1990s, in LIGHT, P., SHELDON, S. and WOODHEAD, M. (eds) *Child Development in Social Context 2. Learning to Think,* London, Routledge in association with the Open University.

DAVIES, B. (1989) *Frogs and Snails and Feminist Tales. Preschool Children and Gender,* Sydney, Allen and Unwin.

DAVIES, D. (1981) *Popular Culture, Class, and Schooling,* London, Open University Press.

DAVIES, M. (1989) *Get The Picture! Developing visual literacy in the infant classroom,* Birmingham, Development Education Centre.

DAVIS, A. (1982) *Women, Race and Class,* London, Women's Press.

DEARDEN, R.F. (1968) *The Philosophy of Primary Education,* London, Routledge and Kegan Paul.

DEVELOPMENT EDUCATION CENTRE (1986) *Behind the Scenes: Photographs and Inservice Activities for Exploring the Hidden Curriculum,* Birmingham, Development Education Centre.

DEVELOPMENT EDUCATION CENTRE (1989) *Working Now: Photographs and Activities for Exploring Gender Roles in the Primary Classroom,* Birmingham, Development Education Centre.

DEPARTMENT OF EDUCATION AND SCIENCE (1975) *A Language for Life (The Bullock Report),* London, HMSO

DEPARTMENT OF EDUCATION AND SCIENCE (1977) *Education in Schools: a consultative document,* London, HMSO.

DEPARTMENT OF EDUCATION AND SCIENCE (1987) *The National Curriculum 5 —16: A Consultation Document,* London, DES/Welsh Office.

DEPARTMENT OF EDUCATION AND SCIENCE and WELSH OFFICE (1989) *English in the National Curriculum,* London, H.M.S.O.

DE VESEY,C.(1990) *Shared Learning: an active approach to the infant curriculum,* Birmingham, Development Education Centre.

DICKINSON, P. (1982) Facts and figures: some myths in TIERNEY, J. (ed) *Race, Migration and Schooling,* London, Holt, Rinehart and Winston.

DODGSON, P. and STEWART, D. (1981) Multiculturalism or Anti- Racist Teaching: A Question of Alternatives, Multiracial Education, 9, 3, pp. 41-51.

DONALDSON, M. (1978) *Childrens Minds,* London, Fontana Press.

DUNN, J. (1988) *The Beginnings of Social Understanding,* Oxford, Blackwell.

EDWARDS, D. and MERCER, N. (1989) *Common Knowledge. The Development of Understanding in the Classroom,* London, Routledge (first published in 1987 by Methuen).

EGGLESTON, J. (1990) Can anti-racist education survive the 1988 Education Act?, Multicultural Teaching, 8, 3, pp 9-11.

EPSTEIN, D. (1989a) Burnage and after, *Multicultural Education Review,* 9, pp. 31-32, Birmingham, City of Birmingham Education Department.

EPSTEIN, D. (1989b) Teaching about South Africa, *Multicultural Education Review,* 9, pp. 6-9, Birmingham, City of Birmingham Education Department.

EPSTEIN, D. (1991a) Changing Classroom Cultures: an examination of anti-racist pedagogies, INSET and school change in the context of local and national politics, unpublished Ph.D. thesis, University of Birmingham.

EPSTEIN, D. (1991b) Inservice fairy tales? the role and limitations of antiracist INSET, *Multicultural Teaching,* 9, 3, pp. 36-39.

EPSTEIN, D. (1992) An ERA of accountability? Equality and the Education Reform Act, paper given at CEDAR International Conference, Warwick University.

EPSTEIN, D. (ed) (forthcoming) *Straight and Narrow: Lesbian and Gay Issues in Education,* Buckingham, Open University Press.

EPSTEIN, D. (forthcoming) Democratising accountability in education, *British Educational Research Journal.*

EPSTEIN, D. and SEALEY, A. (1990) *Where it Really Matters ... Developing Anti-racist Education in Predominantly White Primary Schools,* Birmingham, Development Education Centre.

FAIRCLOUGH, N. (1989) *Language and Power,* London, Longman.

FANON, F. (1986) *Black Skins, White Masks (trans. C.L.Markmann),* London, Pluto (first published in 1952 as *Peau Noire, Masques Blancs).*

FLETCHER, C., CAREN, M. and WILLIAMS, W. (1985) *Schools on Trial, Milton Keynes,* Open University Press.

FOUCAULT, M (1977) *Discipline and Punish. The Birth of the Prison,* (trans. Alan Sheridan) London, Penguin (first published 1975 as *Surveillir et punir:* Naissance de la prison).

FOUCAULT, M (1978) *The History of Sexuality, Volume 1, An Introduction,* (trans. Hurley, R.) Harmondsworth, Penguin (first published 1976 as La Volonte de savoir).

FRANKLIN, S., LURY, C. and STACEY, J. (eds) (1991) *Off-Centre: Feminism and Cultural Studies,* London, Harper Collins.

FULLAN, M. (1985) Change process and strategies at local level, *Elementary School Journal,* 85,3, pp. 391-421.

FULLAN, M. (1987) Implementing the implementation plan in WIDEEN, M. and ANDREWS, I. (eds) (1987) *Staff Development for School Improvement*, Lewes, Falmer Press.

GABRIEL, J. (1989) Developing Anti-Racist Strategies in ALCOCK, P., GAMBLE, A., GOUGH, I., LEE, P. and WALKER, A. (eds) (1989) *The Social Economy and the Democratio State. A New Policy Agenda*, London, Lawrence and Wishart.

GAINE, C. (1987) *No Problem Here. A Practical Approach to Education and Race in White Schools*, London, Hutchinson.

GALTON, M., SIMON, B., and CROLL, P. (1980) *Inside the Primary Classroom*, London, Routledge and Kegan Paul.

GIFFORD A., Q.C. (1986) *The Broadwater Farm Inquiry, report of an inquiry chaired by A. Gifford, Q.C.*, London, NCCL.

GIFFORD A., Q.C. (1988) *Broadwater Farm Revisited, second report of an inquiry chaired by A. Gifford, Q.C.*, London, NCCL.

GIROUX, H. A. (1983) *Theory and Resistance in Education: a Pedagogy for the Opposition, London*, Heinemann Educational.

GLEESON, D. (1989) *The Paradox of Training*, Milton Keynes, Open University Press.

GOLD, A., BOWE, R. and BALL, S.J. (1990) Special Educational Needs in a new context: micropolitics, money, and Education for All, paper given at BERA Conference.

GOMEZ, J. and SMITH, B. (1990) Talking About It: Homophobia in the Black Community, *Feminist Review*, 34, pp 47-55.

GORDON, P. (1990) A dirty war: the New Right and Local Authority anti-racism in BALL, W. and SOLOMOS, J. (eds) (1990) *Race and Local Politics*, London, Macmillan.

GOULD, S. J. (1984) *The Mismeasure of Man*, Harmondsworth, Penguin (first published, 1981, USA, W.W. Norton & Co. Inc).

GRAMSCI, A. (1971) *Selections from the Prison Notebooks*, ed. and trans. by Q. Hoare and G. Nowell-Smith, London, Lawrence and Wishart.

GRAY, J. and SATTERLY, D. (1976) A chapter of errors: teaching styles and pupil progress in retrospect, *Educational Research*, 19, 1.

GRAY J. and SATTERLY, D. (1981) Formal or informal? A re assessment of the British evidence, *British Journal of Educational Psychology*, 51, 2, pp. 187-196.

GRUGEON, E. and WOODS, P. (1990) *Educating All: Multicultural Perspectives in the Primary School*, London, Routledge.

HALL, S. (1980) Teaching race in JAMES, A. & JEFFCOATE, R., (eds) (1981), *The School in the Multicultural Society*, London, Open University in association with Harper Row.

HALL, S. (1988) The Toad in the Garden: Thatcherism among the Theorists, in NELSON, C. and GROSSBERG, L. (eds), *Marxism and the Interpretation of Culture*, London, Macmillan.

HALL, S. and JEFFERSON, T. (1975) *Resistance Through Rituals. Youth Subcultures in Post-War Britain*, London, Hutchinson in association with the Centre for Contemporary Cultural Studies.

BIBLIOGRAPHY

HALSEY A.H. (1975) Sociology and the equality debate in SCHOOL AND SOCIETY COURSE TEAM AT THE OPEN UNIVERSITY (eds) (1977) (2nd edition) *School and Society: a Sociological Reader,* London, Routledge and Kegan Paul in association with the Open University Press.

HARDING, S. (1991) *Whose Science? Whose Knowledge? Thinking from Women's Lives,* Buckingham, Open University Press.

HARGREAVES, A. (1989) Decomprehensivisation in HARGREAVES, A. and REYNOLDS, D. (eds) (1989), *Education Policies: Controversies and Critiques,* Lewes, Falmer Press.

HARWOOD, D. (1986) To advocate or educate? *Education* 3-13, 14, 1, pp. 51-57.

HATCHER, R. (1985a) Education for racial equality, *Multiracial Education,* 13, 1, pp. 30-46.

HATCHER, R. (1985b) Some comments on Chris Mullard's papers for NAME, paper given at NAME Conference.

HATCHER, R. (1990) Labour's classless policies for schools, *Socialist Outlook,* 23, pp. 28-29.

HATCHER, R. and SHALLICE, J. (1983) The politics of anti-racist education, *Multiracial Education,* 12, 1, pp. 3-21.

HENRIQUES, J. (1984) Social psychology and the politics of racism in HENRIQUES, J., HOLLWAY, W., URWIN, C., VENN, C. and WALKERDINE, V. *Changing the Subject. Psychology, Social regulation and Subjectivity,* London, Methuen.

HENRIQUES, J., HOLLWAY, W., URWIN, C., VENN, C. and WALKERDINE, V. (1984) *Changing the Subject. Psychology, Social regulation and Subjectivity,* London, Methuen.

HESSARI, R. and HILL, D. (1989) *Practical Ideas for Multi cultural Learning and Teaching in the Primary Classroom,* London, Routledge.

HILLCOLE GROUP (1991) Critique of Alternative Policies in CHITTY, C. (ed) *Changing the Future: RedPrint for Education,* London, Tufnell Press.

Hodgeon, J. (1985) *A womans world?, in LANGUAGE AND GENDER WORKING PARTY, Alice in Genderland,* London, NATE publications.

HOOKS, B. (1982) *Ain't I a Woman. Black Women and Feminism,* London, Pluto Press.

HOOKS, B. (1989) *Talking Back: thinking feminist, thinking black,* London, Sheba Feminist Publishers.

HOPKINS, D. (1986) The change process and leadership in schools, School Organization, 6,1, pp 81-100.

HOPKINS, D.(1987) *Improving the Quality of Schooling,* Lewes, Falmer Press.

HUGHES, M. (1975) Egocentrism in Pre-School Children, unpublished Ph.D. thesis, Edinburgh University.

HUGHES, M. (1986) *Children and Number: Difficulties in Learning Mathematics,* Oxford, Blackwell.

HUTCHINS, P. (1970), *Rosie's Walk,* London, Bodley Head (paperback edition, Puffin Books).

INGLEBY, D. (1986) Development in social context, in RICHARDS, M. and LIGHT, P. (eds), *Children of Social Worlds*, Cambridge, Polity Press.

ISSUES IN RACE AND EDUCATION (1984), Rehana's Reception, *Issues in Race and Education*, Autumn 1984, London, ILEA.

JEFFCOATE, R. (1979) *Positive Image: Towards a Multiracial Curriculum*, London, Writers and Readers.

JEFFCOATE, R. (1981) Evaluating the multicultural curriculum: pupils' perspectives in JAMES, A. and JEFFCOATE, R. (eds) *The School in the Multicultural Society*, London, Harper & Row/Open University Press.

JEFFCOATE, R. (1984) *Ethnic Minorities and Education*, London, Harper and Row.

JOHN, G. (1986) *The Black Working Class Movement in Education and Schooling and the 1985-86 Teachers Dispute* (pamphlet), London, The Black Parents Movement.

JOHNSON, R. (1991a) A new road to serfdom? A critical history of the 1988 Act in CULTURAL STUDIES, BIRMINGHAM *Education Limited: Schooling, Training and the New Right Since 1979*, London, Unwin Hyman.

JOHNSON, R. (1991b) My New Right education in CULTURAL STUDIES, BIRMINGHAM *Education Limited: Schooling,Training and the New Right Since 1979*, London, Unwin Hyman.

JONES, K. (1989) *Right Turn: the Conservative Revolution in Education*, London, Hutchinson Radius.

JONES, K. (1990a) Equality and the National Curriculum, *Multicultural Teaching*, 8, 3, pp 16-17.

JONES, K. (1990b) The National Curriculum: working for hegemony, paper given at BERA Conference.

KELLY, E. and COHN, T. (1988) *Racism in Schools — new research evidence*, Stoke-on-Trent, Trentham Books.

KELLY, L., REGAN, L. and BURTON, S. (1991) An Exploratory Study of the Prevalence of Sexual Abuse in a Sample of 16-21 Year Olds, (mimeograph) Child Abuse Studies Unit, Polytechnic of North London.

KERR, J. (1968) *The Tiger Who Came To Tea, London,* Picture Lions.

KING, E. (1986) Recent experimental strategies for prejudice in American schools and classrooms, *Journal of Curriculum Studies,* 18, 3, pp 331-338.

KING, R. (1978) *All Things Bright and Beautiful? A Sociological Study of Infants Classrooms,* London, Wiley.

KIRP, D. (1979) *Doing Good By Doing Little, London,* University of California Press.

KLEIN, G. (1985) *Reading into Racism. Bias in children's literature and learning materials,* London, Routledge and Kegan Paul.

KLEIN, G. (1986) Resources for multicultural education in ARORA, R. and DUNCAN, C. (eds) *Multicultural Education: towards good practice,* London, Routledge and Kegan Paul.

LABOUR PARTY (1990) *Looking to the Future, London,* The Labour Party.

LANE, J. (1984) Childcare shapes the future — the need for an anti-racist strategy, *Education Journal,* 6, 2, pp. 2-4.

LANGUAGE AND GENDER WORKING PARTY (1985) *Alice in Genderland*, London, NATE publications.

LEE, V. and LEE, J. with PEARSON, M. (1987) Stories children tell in POLLARD, A. (ed) *Children and Their Primary Schools. A New Perspective*, London, Falmer Press.

LIGHT, P. (1991) Learning to think in WOODHEAD, M. and LIGHT, P., *E820, Child Development in Social Context. Study Guide*, Milton Keynes, Open University.

LIGHT, P. and PERRET-CLERMONT, A-N. (1989) Social context effects in learning and testing in LIGHT, P., SHELDON, S. and WOODHEAD, M. (eds)(1991) *Child development in Social Context 2. Learning to Think*, London, Routledge in association with the Open University.

LLOYD, E., PHOENIX, A. and WOOLLETT, A. (eds) (1991) *Social Construction of Motherhood*, London, Sage.

LOBBAN, G. (1974) Sex roles in reading schemes in WEINER, G. and ARNOT, M. (eds) (1987), *Gender Under Scrutiny: New Inquiries in Education*, London, Hutchinson.

LYSEIGHT-JONES, P. (1989) A management of change perspective in COLE, M. (ed) *Education for Equality. Some Guidelines for Good Practice*, London, Routledge.

MACDONALD,B. (1973) Innovation and incompetence in HAMINGTON, D. (ed), *Towards Judgement: the Publications of the Evaluation Unit of the Humanities Curriculum Project 1970-72*, Occasional Publication 1, Centre for Applied Research in Education, University of East Anglia.

MACDONALD, I., BHAVNANI, R., KHAN, L., JOHN, G. (1989) *Murder in the Playground: the Report of the Macdonald Inquiry into Racism and Racial Violence in Manchester schools*, London, Longsight.

McINTYRE, D. (1976) Teaching styles and pupil progress: a review of Bennett's study, *British Journal of Teacher Education*, 2,3, pp.291-7 (Reprinted in HAMMERSLEY M. (ed) (1986) *Case Studies in Classroom Research*, Milton Keynes, Open University Press).

McKINNON, C.A. (1987) Feminism, Marxism, Method and the State. Toward Feminist Jurisprudence in HARDING, S. (ed) *Feminism and Methodology, Bloomington and Milton Keynes, Indiana University Press and Open University Press*.

McPHAIL, P., UNGOED-THOMAS, J.R. and CHAPMAN, H. (1972) *Moral Education in Secondary Schools, Schools Council Project in Moral Education, London, Longman*.

MILLER, A. (1979 — German edition, 1988 — English edition), The Drama of Being a Child, London, Virago.

MILLER, H.J. (1967) A study of the effectiveness of a variety of teaching techniques for reducing colour prejudice in a male student sample aged 15-21, unpublished M.A. dissertation, London University.

MILNER, D. (1983) *Children and Race Ten Years On, London, Ward Lock Educational.*

MULLARD, C. (1981) Multiracial education in Britain: from assimilation to cultural pluralism in TIERNEY, J. (ed) (1982), Race, Migration and Schooling, London, Holt, Rinehart and Winston.

MULLARD, C. (1984) *Anti-Racist Education: The Three Os, Walsall, NAME.*

NAIDOO, B. (1985) *Journey to Joburg: a South African Story, Harlow, Longman.*

NAIDOO, B. (1989) *Chain of Fire, London, Collins.*

NAIDOO, B. (1990), Exploring issues of racism with white students through literature, paper given at BERA Conference.

NAIDOO, B. (1991) Exploring issues of racism with white students through a literature based course, unpublished Ph.D. thesis, University of Southampton.

NAIDOO, B. (1992) *Through Whose Eyes? Exploring racism: reader, text and context*, Stoke-on-Trent, Trentham Books.

NAME (1985) *NAME on Swann, Walsall*, NAME.

NATIONAL CURRICULUM COUNCIL (1988a) *Mathematics for Ages 5 to 16*, London, DES/Welsh Office.

NATIONAL CURRICULUM COUNCIL (1988b) *English for Ages 5 to 11*, London, D.E.S./Welsh Office (The Cox Report 1).

NATIONAL CURRICULUM COUNCIL (1988c) *Task Group on Assessment and Testing: A Report*, London, D.E.S./Welsh Office (TGAT Report).

NATIONAL CURRICULUM COUNCIL (1989) *English for Ages 5-16*, London, DES/Welsh Office (the 2nd Cox Report).

NATIONAL CURRICULUM COUNCIL (1990) *Curriculum Guidance 8. Education for Citizenship*, York, NCC.

NIXON, J. (1985) *A Teacher's Guide to Multicultural Education*, Oxford, Basil Blackwell.

NATIONAL UNION OF TEACHERS (1986) *Education for Equality: the National Union of Teachers Response to the Swann Report*, London, NUT.

O'HEAR, A. (1988) *Who Teaches the Teachers? A Contribution to Public Debate*, London, Social Affairs Unit.

OPEN UNIVERSITY (1986) *E333, Policy Making in Education*, Milton Keynes, Open University Press.

OXFORD REVIEW OF EDUCATION (1991) *Special Issue: Equality and Education Revisited*, 17, 2.

OZGA, J. (1986) The Policy-Makers in OPEN UNIVERSITY (1986), E333 *Policy-Making in Education, Module 2: The Policy-Makers: Local and Central Government*, Milton Keynes, Open University Press.

PALEY, V.G. (1987) *Wally's Stories*, Cambridge, Mass., Harvard University Press.

PALMER, F. (ed) (1986) *Anti-Racism — An Assault on Education and Value*, London, Sherwood Press.

PAREKH, B. (1986), The concept of multi-cultural education in MODGIL, S., VERMA, G.K., MALLICK, K. and MODGIL, C. (eds) (1986), *Multi-Cultural Education: The Interminable Debate*, Lewes, Falmer Press.

PARMAR, P. (1982) Gender, race and class: Asian women in resistance in CENTRE FOR CONTEMPORARY CULTURAL STUDIES *The Empire Strikes Back*, London, Hutchinson.

PHILLIPS-BELL, M. (1981) Multiracial Education: What is it? *Multiracial Education*, 10, 1, pp.21-26.

PIAGET, J. (1926) *The Language and Thought of the Child*, London, Routledge and Kegan Paul.

PIAGET, J. (1932) *The Moral Judgement of the Child*, London, Routledge and Kegan Paul.

PIAGET, J. and INHELDER, B. (1969) *The Psychology of the Child*, London, Routledge and Kegan Paul.

POLLARD, A. (ed) (1987) *Children and Their Primary Schools. A New Perspective*, Lewes, Falmer Press.

POLLARD, A. and TANN, C.S. (1987) *Reflective Teaching in the Primary School*, London, Cassell.

RABINOW, P. (ed) (1984) *The Foucault Reader. An introduction to Foucault's thought*, London, Penguin.

RAMPTON, B. (1989/90) Some unofficial perspectives on bilingualism and education for all, *Language Issues*, 3, 2, pp. 27-32.

REEVE, A. (1981) The Way Forward or The Long and Winding Road?, *Multiracial Education*, 9, 3, pp. 35-40.

REYNOLDS, K. (1990) Education in London after ILEA: Equal Opportunities and Social Justice, paper given at BERA Conference (published 1991 as Restructuring the Welfare State — the case of the abolition of the Inner London Education Authority, *Critical Social Policy*, 32, pp 72-81).

RICH, A. (1983) *Compulsory Heterosexuality and Lesbian Existence*, London, Only-women Press.

RICHARDSON, R (1985) Each and every school: responding, reviewing, planning and doing, *Multicultural Teaching*, 3, 3.

RICHARDSON, R (1990) For Those Who Remain: A Personal Memoir of Brent, 1985-1990, unpublished.

ROGERS, C. (1983) *Freedom to Learn for the 80s*, Columbus and London, Bell & Howell.

ROGERS, V.R. and BARRON, J. (1976) Questioning the evidence,*TES*, 30 April, pp. 20-21.

ROSE, S. (1987) *Molecules and Minds*, Milton Keynes, Open University Press.

ROSE, S., LEWONTIN, R.C. and KAMIN, L.J. (1984) *Not in Our Genes*, Harmondsworth, Penguin.

ROUSSEAU, J.J. (1762; 1963) *Emile* (trans. Foxley, B.), London, Dent.

RUSHIN, D.K. (1981) The Bridge Poem in MORAGA, C. and ANZALDUA, G.(eds) (2nd ed. 1983) *This Bridge Called My Back. Writings by Radical Women of Color*, New York, Kitchen Table: Women of Color Press.

SCRUTON, R (1986) The myth of cultural relativism in PALMER, F. (ed) *Anti-Racism —an Assault on Education and Value*, London, Sherwood Press.

SEALEY, A.(1990) Magic words: helping young children to develop their Knowledge about Language, in CARTER, R. (ed) *Knowledge about Language and the Curriculum: The LINC Reader*, London, Hodder and Stoughton.

SEXTON, S. (1987) *Our Schools: A Radical Policy*, Warlingham, IEA, Education Unit.

SHAW, B (1987) Teacher Training: The Misdirection of British Teaching in O'Keeffe, D. *The Wayward Curriculum*, London, Social Affairs Unit.

SHORT, G. (1988) Children's grasp of controversial issues, in CARRINGTON, B. and TROYNA, B. (eds) *Children and Controversial Issues,* Lewes, Falmer.

SHORT, G. and CARRINGTON, B. (1987) Towards an anti-racist initiative in the all-white primary school in POLLARD, A. (ed) *Children and Their Primary Schools: A New Perspective,* Lewes, Falmer.

SINGH, B. (1988) The teaching of controversial issues: the problems of the neutral-chair approach, in CARRINGTON, B. and TROYNA, B. (eds) *Children and Controversial Issues,* Lewes, Falmer.

SIRAJ-BLATCHFORD, I. (1991) A study of black students' perceptions of racism in Initial Teacher Education, *British Educational Research Journal,* 17, 1, pp 35-50.

SMITH, D.J. and TOMLINSON, S. (1990) *The School Effect: A Study of a Multiracial Comprehensive,* London, Policy Studies Institute.

SMITH, F. (1978) *Reading,* Cambridge, Cambridge University Press.

SMITH, M. (1983) *The Libertarians in Education,* London, Unwin. Education Books.

SPENDER, D. (1980) *Man Made Language,* London, Routledge and Kegan Paul.

STACEY, J. (1991) Promoting normality: Section 28 and the regulation of sexuality in FRANKLIN, S., LURY, C. and STACEY, J. (eds) *Off-Centre: Feminism and Cultural Studies,* London, Harper Collins Academic.

STEEDMAN, C., URWIN, C. and WALKERDINE, V. (eds) (1985) *Language, Gender and Childhood,* London, Routledge and Kegan Paul.

STENHOUSE, L. (ed) (1980) *Curriculum Research and Development,* London, Heinemann Educational.

STENHOUSE, L., VERMA, G.K., WILD, R.D. and NIXON, J. (1982) *Teaching about Race Relations,* London, Routledge and Kegan Paul

STONE, M. (1981) *The Education of the Black Child. The Myth of Multiracial Education,* London, Fontana.

STRAKER-WELDS, M. (ed) (1984) *Education for a Multicultural Society. Case studies in ILEA schools,* London, Bell and Hyman.

STREDDER, K.M.N. (1978) An Illuminative Evaluation of a Piece of Multiracial Curriculum Implemented in a Multiracial Secondary School in Birmingham, unpublished M.Ed. dissertation, Faculty of Education, Birmingham University.

STREDDER, K.M.N. (1987) The Politics of Educational Racism, a Case Study of Educational Policy and Politics in Wolverhampton, unpublished Ph.D. thesis, Wolverhampton Polytechnic.

TIERNEY, J. (ed) (1982) *Race, Migration and Schooling,* London, Holt, Rinehart and Winston.

TIZARD, B. and HUGHES, M. (1984) *Young Children Learning, London, Fontana.*

TIZARD, B., BLATCHFORD, P., BURKE, J., FARQUHAR, C. and PLEWIS, I. (1988) *Young Children and School in the Inner City,* London, Erlbaum.

TOMLINSON, S. and COULSON, P. (1988) Education for a Multi-Ethnic Society: A Descriptive Analysis of a Sample of Projects Funded by Education Support Grants in mainly white areas, (mimeograph) University of Lancaster.

TROYNA, B. (1983) Multiracial education: just another brick in the wall?, in *New Community*, X, 3, pp. 424-428.

TROYNA, B. (1987) Beyond Multiculturalism: towards the enactment of antiracist education in policy, provision and pedagogy, *Oxford Review of Education*, 13, 3, pp. 307-319.

TROYNA, B. and BALL, W. (1985) *Views from the Chalk Face: School Responses to and LEAs Policy on Multicultural Education*, Policy Papers in Ethnic Relations No. 1, Coventry, Centre for Research in Ethnic Relations.

TROYNA, B. and CARRINGTON, B. (1990) *Education, Racism and Reform*, London, Routledge.

TROYNA, B. and HATCHER, R. (1992) *Racism in children's lives. A study of mainly-white primary schools*, London, Routledge.

TROYNA, B. and WILLIAMS, J. (1986) *Racism, Education and the State*, London, Croom Helm.

TRUDGILL, P. (1975) *Accent, Dialect and the School*, London, Edward Arnold.

URWIN, C (1984) Power relations and the emergence of language in HENRIQUES, J., HOLLWAY, W., URWIN, C., VENN, C. and WALKERDINE, V, *Changing the Subject. Psychology, Social Regulation and Subjectivity*, London, Methuen.

VYGOTSKY, L.S. (1962) *Thought and Language*, Cambridge, MIT Press (originally published 1934).

VYGOTSKY, L.S. (1966) Genesis of the higher mental functions, in LIGHT, P., SHELDON, S. and WOODHEAD, M. (1991) (eds) *Learning to Think*, London, Routledge in association with the Open University (originally written in 1930-31).

VYGOTSKY, L.S. (1978) *Mind in Society: The Development of Higher Psychological Processes*, Cambridge, Massechusets, Harvard University Press.

WALKER, A. (1967) The civil rights movement: what good was it? in WALKER, A. (1984) *In Search of Our Mothers' Gardens*. Womanist Prose, London, Womens Press.

WALKER, A. (1973) Choice: a tribute to Martin Luther King in WALKER, A. (1984) *In Search of Our Mothers' Gardens*. Womanist Prose, London, Womens Press.

WALKERDINE, V. (1981) Sex, power and pedagogy, *Screen Education*, 38, pp. 14-24 (Reprinted in ARNOT.M. and WEINER, G. (eds) (1987) *Gender and the Politics of Schooling*, London, Hutchinson and in WALKERDINE, V. (1990) *Schoolgirl fictions*, London, Verso).

WALKERDINE, V. (1984) Developmental psychology and the child-centred pedagogy: the insertion of Piaget into early education in HENRIQUES, J., HOLLWAY, W., URWIN, C., VENN, C. and WALKERDINE, V, (1984) *Changing the Subject. Psychology, Social Regulation and Subjectivity*, London, Methuen.

WALKERDINE, V. (1985) On the regulation of speaking and silence: subjectivity, class and gender in contemporary schooling in STEEDMAN, C., URWIN, C. and WALKERDINE, V. (eds) *Language, Gender and Childhood*, London, Routledge and Kegan Paul.

WALKERDINE, V. (1989) (compiled by her for THE GIRLS AND MATHEMATICS UNIT) *Counting Girls Out*, London, Virago.

WALKERDINE, V. (1990) *Schoolgirl Fictions*, London, Verso.

WALKERDINE, V. and LUCEY, H. (1989) *Democracy in the Kitchen: Regulating Mothers and Socialising Daughters,* London, Virago.

WATERLAND, L (1985) *Read With Me. An apprenticeship approach to reading,* Stroud, Thimble Press.

WEEDON, C. (1987) *Feminist Practice and Poststructuralist Theory,* Oxford, Basil Blackwell.

WELLS, G. (1986) *The Meaning Makers: Children Learning Language and Using Language to Learn,* London, Hodder and Stoughton (this edition published in 1987).

WHITEHEAD, F., CAPEY, A.C., MADDREN, W. and WELLINGS, A. (1977) *Children and their Books,* London, Schools Council/Macmillan Educational.

WILLES, M.J. (1983) *Children into Pupils. A study of language in early schooling,* London, Routledge and Kegan Paul.

WILLIS, P. (1976) The class significance of school counter-culture in HAMMERSLEY, M. and WOODS, P. (eds) *The Process of Schooling,* London, Routledge and Kegan Paul.

WILLIS, P. (1977) *Learning to Labour: How Working Class Kids Get Working Class Jobs.* Aldershot, Gower (first published Saxon House).

WOOD, D.J. (1988) *How Children Think and Learn, Oxford,* Blackwell.

WOOD, D.J., BRUNER, J.S. and ROSS, G. (1976) The role of tutoring in problem solving, *Journal of Child Psychology and Psychiatry,* 17, 2, pp. 89-100.

WRIGHT, C. (1986) School processes — an ethnographic study in EGGLESTON, J., DUNN, D. and ANJALI, M. (1986), *Education For Some. The Educational and Vocational Experiences of 15-18 year- old Members of Minority Ethnic Groups,* Stoke-on-Trent, Trentham Books.

YEOMANS, A. (1983) Collaborative group work in primary and secondary schools, *Durham and Newcastle Research Review,* 10, pp. 95-100.

Index